COUNTERLAND OPERATIONS

Air Force Doctrine Document 3-03
11 September 2006

Incorporating Change 1, 28 July 2011

This document complements related discussion found in Joint Publication 3-0, *Joint Operations*; 3-03, *Joint Interdiction*; 3-09, *Joint Fire Support*; and 3-09.3, *Joint Tactics, Techniques, and Procedures for Close Air Support*

Cover Sheet for Air Force Doctrine Document (AFDD) 3-03, *Counterland Operations*

OPR: LeMay Center/DD

28 July 2011

AFDD numbering has changed to correspond with the joint doctrine publication numbering architecture (the AFDD titles remain unchanged until the doctrine is revised). Any AFDD citations within the documents will list the old AFDD numbers until the doctrine is revised. The changed numbers follow:

OLD	NEW	TITLE
AFDD 2-1	changed to AFDD 3-1	*Air Warfare*
AFDD 2-1.1	changed to AFDD 3-01	*Counterair Operations*
AFDD 2-1.2	changed to AFDD 3-70	*Strategic Attack*
AFDD 2-1.3	changed to AFDD 3-03	*Counterland Operations*
AFDD 2-1.4	changed to AFDD 3-04	*Countersea Operations*
AFDD 2-1.6	changed to AFDD 3-50	*Personnel Recovery Operations*
AFDD 2-1.7	changed to AFDD 3-52	*Airspace Control*
AFDD 2-1.8	changed to AFDD 3-40	*Counter-CBRN*
AFDD 2-1.9	changed to AFDD 3-60	*Targeting*
AFDD 2-10	changed to AFDD 3-27	*Homeland Operations*
AFDD 2-12	changed to AFDD 3-72	*Nuclear Operations*
AFDD 2-2	changed to AFDD 3-14	*Space Operations*
AFDD 2-2.1	changed to AFDD 3-14.1	*Counterspace Operations*
AFDD 2-3	changed to AFDD 3-24	*Irregular Warfare*
AFDD 2-3.1	changed to AFDD 3-22	*Foreign Internal Defense*
AFDD 2-4	changed to AFDD 4-0	*Combat Support*
AFDD 2-4.1	changed to AFDD 3-10	*Force Protection*
AFDD 2-4.2	changed to AFDD 4-02	*Health Services*
AFDD 2-4.4	changed to AFDD 4-11	*Bases, Infrastructure, and Facilities* [Rescinded]
AFDD 2-4.5	changed to AFDD 1-04	*Legal Support*
AFDD 2-5	changed to AFDD 3-13	*Information Operations*
AFDD 2-5.1	changed to AFDD 3-13.1	*Electronic Warfare*
AFDD 2-5.3	changed to AFDD 3-61	*Public Affairs Operations*
AFDD 2-6	changed to AFDD 3-17	*Air Mobility Operations*
AFDD 2-7	changed to AFDD 3-05	*Special Operations*
AFDD 2-8	changed to AFDD 6-0	*Command and Control*
AFDD 2-9	changed to AFDD 2-0	*ISR Operations*
AFDD 2-9.1	changed to AFDD 3-59	*Weather Operations*

BY ORDER OF THE
SECRETARY OF THE AIR FORCE

AIR FORCE DOCTRINE DOCUMENT 3-03
11 SEPTEMBER 2006
INCORPORATING CHANGE 1, 28 JULY 2011 |

SUMMARY OF CHANGES

This Interim change to Air Force Doctrine Document (AFDD) 2-1.3 changes the cover to AFDD 3-03, *Counterland Operations* to reflect revised AFI 10-1301, Air Force Doctrine (9 August 2010). AFDD numbering has changed to correspond with the joint doctrine publication numbering architecture. AFDD titles and content remain unchanged until updated in the next full revision. A margin bar indicates newly revised material. changes the cover to avoid confusion and inserts a chart outlining new AFDD numbering. A margin bar indicates newly revised material.

Supersedes: AFDD 2-1.3, 27 August 1999
OPR: LeMay Center/DD
Certified by: LeMay Center/DD (Col Todd C. Westhauser)
Pages: 113
Accessibility: Available on the e-publishing website at www.e-publishing.af.mil for
            downloading
Releasability: There are no releasability restrictions on this publication
Approved by: LeMay Center/CC, Maj Gen Thomas K. Andersen, USAF
            Commander, LeMay Center for Doctrine Development and Education

FOREWORD

In war, defeating an enemy's force is often a necessary step on the path to victory. Defeating enemy armies is a difficult task that often comes with a high price tag in terms of blood and treasure. With its inherent speed, range, and flexibility, air and space power offers a way to lower that risk by providing commanders a synergistic tool that can provide a degree of control over the surface environment and render enemy forces ineffective before they meet friendly land forces. Modern air and space power directly affects an adversary's ability to initiate, conduct, and sustain ground combat.

Counterland operations dominate the surface environment by crushing an enemy's ability to fight on land. Through air interdiction, air and space power can divert, disrupt, delay, or destroy enemy military potential before it can be brought to bear against friendly ground forces, and achieve joint force commander objectives independently. Indeed, the devastation wrought on an enemy by air and space power may preclude costly ground combat. When called for, air and space power delivers devastating support to assist friendly ground forces in achieving their objectives.

Twenty-first century capabilities regarding precision, information technology, space, intelligence, and command and control increase counterland effectiveness. Modern counterland capabilities can help achieve objectives more efficiently than in the past. This provides commanders a flexible capability that makes other applications of military power more effective and may drive an early end to conflict.

When the objective is to destroy an enemy army's capability to fight, air and space power should always be considered as a first option. Air and space power has inherent, unique advantages in conducting counterland operations, but commanders should recognize they are more effective in conjunction with other forms of military action. In fact, other air and space power functions often complement counterland operations to produce operational level effects to destroy an enemy's warfighting capability.

Air Force Doctrine Document 2-1.3, *Counterland Operations*, is doctrine for understanding, planning, and executing this crucial air and space power function across the full range of military operations. Air Force personnel need to be able to articulate the rationale for counterland as a valuable warfighting option for the combatant commander. More importantly, Air Force personnel must understand how counterland operations can help enhance military strategies as a tool for defeating our nation's adversaries.

Allen G. Peck
Major General, USAF
Commander, Headquarters
Air Force Doctrine Center

TABLE OF CONTENTS

INTRODUCTION

PURPOSE

This Air Force doctrine document (AFDD) establishes doctrinal guidance for the United States Air Force on counterland. It articulates fundamental Air Force principles for the application of combat force and provides commanders operational guidance on the employment and integration of Air Force resources to achieve desired objectives.

APPLICATION

This AFDD applies to the Total Force: all Air Force military and civilian personnel, including regular, Air Force Reserve, and Air National Guard units and members. Unless specifically stated otherwise, Air Force doctrine applies to the full range of military operations.

The doctrine in this document is authoritative, but not directive. Therefore, commanders need to consider the contents of this AFDD and the particular situation when accomplishing their missions. Airmen should read it, discuss it, and practice it.

SCOPE

This doctrine provides guidance for planning and conducting counterland operations in support of US national security and combatant/joint force commander objectives.

COMAFFOR / JFACC / CFACC
A note on terminology

One of the cornerstones of Air Force doctrine is that "the US Air Force prefers - and in fact, plans and trains - to employ through a commander, Air Force forces (COMAFFOR) who is also dual-hatted as a joint force air and space component commander (JFACC)." (AFDD 1)

To simplify the use of nomenclature, Air Force doctrine documents will assume the COMAFFOR is dual-hatted as the JFACC unless specifically stated otherwise. The term "COMAFFOR" refers to the Air Force Service component commander while the term "JFACC" refers to the joint component-level operational commander.

While both joint and Air Force doctrine state that one individual will normally be dual-hatted as COMAFFOR and JFACC, the two responsibilities are different, and should be executed through different staffs.

Normally, the COMAFFOR function executes operational control/administrative control of assigned and attached Air Force forces through a Service A-staff while the JFACC function executes tactical control of joint air and space component forces through an air and space operations center (AOC).

When multinational operations are involved, the JFACC becomes a combined force air and space component commander (CFACC). Likewise, the air and space operations center, though commonly referred to as an AOC, in joint or combined operations is correctly known as a JAOC or CAOC. Since nearly every operation the US conducts will involve international partners, this publication uses the terms CFACC and CAOC throughout to emphasize the doctrine's applicability to multi-national operations.

FOUNDATIONAL DOCTRINE STATEMENTS

Foundational doctrine statements are the basic principles and beliefs upon which AFDDs are built. Other information in the AFDDs expands on or supports these statements.

- ✪ Counterland operations are air and space operations against enemy land force capabilities to create effects that achieve joint force commander (JFC) objectives (Page 1)

- ✪ Counterland operations are a form of maneuver warfare that seeks to shatter an enemy's fighting ability through focused attacks against key enemy military targets. (Page 2)

- ✪ Counterland operations can serve as the main attack and be the decisive means for achieving JFC objectives. (Page 3)

- ✪ Counterland operations can achieve tactical-, operational-, or strategic-level effects, and can significantly influence the course of a military operation. (Page 4)

- ✪ Counterland operations are supported by two types of air operations for engaging enemy land forces: air interdiction (AI) and close air support (CAS). (Page 5)

- ✪ The Air Force defines AI as air operations conducted to divert, disrupt, delay, or destroy the enemy's military potential before it can be brought to bear against friendly forces or to otherwise achieve JFC objectives. These operations are conducted at such distance from friendly forces that detailed integration with those forces is not required. (Page 5)

- ✪ The combined force air and space component commander (CFACC) is normally the supported commander for the JFC's overall AI effort. When designated as the supported commander, the CFACC will conduct theater-wide or joint operations area-wide AI in direct support of the JFC's overall theater objectives. (Page 6)

- ✪ CAS is air action by fixed- and rotary-winged aircraft against hostile targets that are in close proximity to friendly forces and which require detailed integration of each air mission with the fire and movement of those forces. (Page 6)

- ✪ AI can channel movements, constrict logistic systems, disrupt communications, force urgent movement, and attrit enemy fielded forces. (Page 21)

✪ Accurate information about the enemy's support characteristics, force structure, and ability to adapt is imperative to successful AI. (Page 30)

✪ The success of both offensive and defensive CAS operations in contiguous, linear warfare may depend on massing effects at decisive points—not diluting them across the entire battlefield. (Page 33)

✪ Missions attacking targets not in close proximity to friendly forces, and beyond the range requiring detailed integration with surface fires and maneuver, should be conducted using AI procedures vice CAS. (Page 38)

✪ Throughout the entire process, CAS operations remain under the control of the joint air component while supporting the joint land component. (Page 50)

✪ The theater air control system (TACS) provides the CFACC the capability to centrally plan and control joint air operations through the combined air operations center while facilitating decentralized execution through the subordinate elements of the TACS. (Page 51)

✪ The preponderance of kinetic effects shifts from landpower to airpower near the maximum range of organic field artillery. Therefore, under all but the most rapid ground maneuvers, the fire support coordination line (FSCL) is normally placed near the maximum range of tube artillery because air and space power provides the most expeditious attack of surface targets beyond that point. (Page 70)

✪ The FSCL is primarily used to establish command and control procedures for planning and execution purposes—it does not define mission types. (Page 71)

CHAPTER ONE

COUNTERLAND FUNDAMENTALS

> *The air force has become the hammer of modern warfare on land... aviation gives modern battle a third dimension.*
>
> **— Lieutenant Colonel Ferdinand Otto Miksche, Infantry Officer & Military Strategist, writing in 1942**

Military history provides many successful examples where airpower smashed enemy land forces in modern warfare, from the breakout of Normandy in World War II to the destruction of the Iraqi army in 1991 and 2003. Attacking the capabilities of land forces through air and space power—counterland operations—is often a necessary step on the path to military victory. As a vital element in joint warfare, air and space power continues to demonstrate a unique ability to accurately find, fix, track, target, engage, and assess (F2T2EA) enemy land forces. Because of these essential counterland capabilities, it is virtually unthinkable to go into combat without air and space power today. With a solid comprehension of counterland operations, Airmen increase their ability to properly plan and execute air warfare against enemy land forces. This chapter provides a basis for understanding counterland operations by giving a fundamental explanation of its purpose, functional missions, and capabilities.

DEFINITION AND PURPOSE

Counterland operations are air and space operations against enemy land force capabilities to create effects that achieve joint force commander (JFC) objectives. The aim of counterland operations is to dominate the surface environment using air and space power. By dominating the surface environment, counterland operations can assist friendly land maneuver while denying the enemy the ability to resist. Although most frequently associated with support to friendly surface forces, counterland operations may also be conducted independent of friendly surface force objectives or in operations where no friendly land forces are present. For example, recent conflicts in the Balkans, Afghanistan, and Iraq illustrate situations where counterland operations have been used absent significant friendly land forces or with small numbers of special operations forces (SOF) providing target cueing. This independent or direct attack of adversary land operations by air and space forces often provides the key to success when seizing the initiative, especially in the opening phase of an operation.

The JFC has two distinct means for engaging enemy land forces that support counterland operations. The first is air interdiction (AI), in which airpower supports land forces in addition to supporting JFC objectives. The second method is close air support (CAS), in which airpower directly supports land maneuver. Whether destroying enemy surface forces, interdicting supply routes, or providing CAS to friendly troops, counterland operations are a vital air and space power function that applies throughout the range of conflict.

Counterland operations are a form of aerial maneuver that seeks to shatter an enemy's fighting ability through focused attacks against key enemy military targets. Air and space forces, with their inherent speed, range, and precision attack capabilities, are superior theater-level maneuver forces. Where ground forces must seek out weak points in the enemy line to penetrate and exploit, aircraft and missiles can maneuver in three dimensions and directly attack key points in the enemy rear. By striking enemy military targets such as fielded land forces, command and control (C2) nodes, vital logistics, or supporting infrastructure, the destruction of decisive points, forces, and capabilities degrades the enemy system and ultimately renders the enemy incapable of effective resistance. Persistently applied, airpower can permanently disrupt the enemy and crush its ability to fight as a coherent, effective whole, thus wresting initiative and dictating tempo.

Counterland operations can support and facilitate maneuver warfare on land. World War I saw the first widespread use of airpower in support of Allied land operations when combat aircraft began cutting supply routes, strafing trenches, and bombing fielded forces. Military leaders soon realized that airpower added a synergistic element to conventional ground forces because of its ability to attack behind enemy lines and support offensive breakthroughs. Since then, counterland operations have occurred in every major war as well as numerous smaller conflicts characterized by protracted, low-intensity conflict. In each instance, air and space power's ability to maneuver in three dimensions has proven invaluable in supporting friendly surface maneuvers by destroying, disrupting, delaying, or denying an enemy's operational military potential.

Counterland operations achieve JFC objectives. In the first week of November 2001; bombers and fighters supported by SOF destroyed Taliban forces defending the enemy stronghold of Mazar-i-Sharif during Operation ENDURING FREEDOM. These actions facilitated the Northern Alliance's capture of the town on 9 November 2001. Soon, counterland airpower cued by SOF teams routed Taliban forces throughout Afghanistan until Kabul itself fell just days after Mazar-i-Sharif. Within two weeks, Coalition forces took control of Afghanistan by relying on the powerful combination of counterland airpower and distributed ground forces using small-unit tactics.

Counterland operations can serve as the main attack and be the decisive means for achieving JFC objectives. Although often associated with support to friendly surface forces, counterland operations also include operations that directly support theater strategy rather than exclusively supporting a surface component. In some cases, counterland operations can provide the sole effort against the enemy. This occurred in the Balkans during Operation ALLIED FORCE in 1999, when the US-led coalition contained no significant land component. In concert with strategic attack operations, the North Atlantic Treaty Organization's (NATO) independent counterland battle against Serbian ground forces helped end Slobodan Milosevic's ethnic cleansing campaign. In other campaigns where a "boots on the ground" presence is required to achieve the desired end state, counterland operations can decisively engage adversary fielded forces prior to occupation by friendly ground forces. During Operation DESERT STORM, counterland operations broke the back of the Iraqi army and achieved JFC objectives aimed at weakening enemy forces prior to the start of the ground campaign—a fight that lasted only four days. In the end, the devastating effects of counterland operations paved a path for Coalition forces to roll back a demoralized Iraqi army in Kuwait. These recent historical examples illustrate that directly attacking adversary land forces with air and space forces can permit rapid control over the battlefield during early phases of a conflict.

> *Two contrasting historical examples of air warfare illustrate how technology enhances counterland operations. In December 1944, adverse weather prevented Allied airpower from detecting and attacking German Panzer divisions during the initial phases of the Ardennes counteroffensive that ultimately culminated in the Battle of the Bulge. Today, technological advances in air and space power enhance the ability to cope with adverse weather conditions during counterland operations. When a sandstorm struck during Operation IRAQI FREEDOM (OIF), Iraqi leadership perceived an opportunity to attack American ground forces advancing to Baghdad under the cover of foul weather. However, intelligence, surveillance, and reconnaissance (ISR) platforms observed the enemy movement and relayed the information to the combined air and space operations center (CAOC). Using the information transmitted from the CAOC and ISR assets, counterland aircraft soon picked up and identified the moving Republican Guard units. Employing advanced on-board sensors and inertially aided munitions, fighters and bombers interdicted enemy tanks, artillery, and vehicles before they could affect coalition ground forces.*

Air and space power offers a critical capability to deliver lethal and nonlethal combat power against enemy land forces. Due to its inherent speed, range, flexibility,

Air and space power offers a critical capability to deliver lethal and nonlethal combat power against enemy land forces. Due to its inherent speed, range, flexibility, lethality, precision, and ability to mass at a desired time and place, air and space power transcends the normal operating limitations imposed on surface forces. Able to strike enemy surface forces across the width and depth of the theater, air and space power contributes significantly to the counterland effort and can reduce or even eliminate the need to engage in potentially costly ground combat.

Stealth, precision, persistence, information technology, unmanned aircraft system (UAS), and modern sensors have revolutionized counterland warfare. The impressive successes of air and space power during Operations DESERT STORM, ALLIED FORCE, ENDURING FREEDOM, and IRAQI FREEDOM prove the viability of recent technological advances in modern warfare. Stealth and night capabilities increase survivability. Precision weapons enable one sortie to strike several targets rather than requiring several sorties for the destruction of one target. Information technology increases flexibility, aids decision making, facilitates integration, increases tempo, and improves combat assessment during counterland operations. With inherently long loiter and weapons carrying capacity, unmanned aircraft (UA) such as the MQ-1 Predator can provide a persistent counterland capability to the battlefield. Information shared among aircraft, surface forces, command nodes, and space platforms provides valuable intelligence, continuous surveillance, and precise targeting of an enemy's military capabilities. A counterland platform using data link, precision weapons, optical and infrared sensors, radar, and advanced fire control systems provides an all-weather night attack capability that often is equal to, or surpasses, daytime operations in terms of target detection, aircraft survivability, and attack accuracy.

Counterland operations are not strictly associated with a particular type of aircraft or weapon system. Instead, a variety of combat air assets conducts counterland operations to deliver lethal and less than lethal effects against enemy land forces and their support structure. Predominant weapons systems used in counterland operations include aircraft equipped with cannons, bombs, mines, missiles, rockets, and electronic warfare (EW) systems. Air assets, space platforms, and SOF provide intelligence, surveillance, and reconnaissance (ISR) as well as target cueing, navigation aids, and battle damage assessment (BDA). Each weapon system has unique characteristics that should be considered based on the nature of the specific threat, targets to be attacked, and environmental conditions. Many of the assets used to interdict forces deep in the enemy rear can also be used to support the close fight and vice versa. Fighters, bombers, gunships, unmanned aircraft, helicopters, cruise missiles, and Army tactical missile systems (ATACMS) are a few examples of joint assets that air component commanders can use to execute counterland operations.

COUNTERLAND EFFECTS

Counterland operations can achieve tactical-, operational-, or strategic-level effects, and can significantly influence the course of a military operation. Counterland effects focus at the tactical and operational levels of war by targeting fielded enemy surface forces and their supporting infrastructure. When planned and executed successfully, counterland operational effects will indirectly lead to strategic effects by denying the enemy's ability to execute a coherent ground campaign. In cases where the enemy places strategic value on a specific portion of their ground combat force, counterland operations can produce more immediate effects at the strategic level.

As witnessed during the recent conflicts in the Balkans, Iraq, and Afghanistan, *Counterland operations apply across the range of military operations.* Although they are usually associated with history's major wars, counterland operations have routinely taken place in stability operations characterized by insurgency, guerrilla tactics, and civil strife.[1] To be effective, however, counterland operations must adapt to the situation. Conducting counterland operations against an unconventional enemy with a primitive force structure differs from attacking a modern, highly mechanized army with heavy logistics requirements. Therefore, it is crucial to understand the nature of the conflict to properly apply air and space power during counterland operations.

AIR INTERDICTION AND CLOSE AIR SUPPORT

Counterland operations are supported by two types of air operations for engaging enemy land forces: AI and CAS. AI may operate as a supported part of the overall theater strategy or it may indirectly support the land component. CAS is normally considered direct support to surface components by the air component. AI and CAS missions can function under an overall theater posture of offense or defense and are typically coordinated with a ground scheme of maneuver to maximize the effect on the enemy. This section gives a brief overview of AI and CAS by discussing their definitions and purpose to provide a basic understanding of their character. Chapters 2 and 3 expand the discussion and give a more detailed description of each.

Air Interdiction

The purpose of interdiction is to attack the enemy's ability to fight by targeting tactical and operational forces and infrastructure with either lethal or non-lethal means (See Joint Publication [JP] 3-03, *Joint Doctrine for Joint Interdiction*).[2] **The Air Force defines AI as air operations conducted to divert, disrupt, delay, or destroy the enemy's military potential before it can be brought to bear effectively against friendly forces, or to otherwise achieve JFC objectives. AI is conducted at such distance from friendly forces that detailed integration of each air mission with the fire and movement of friendly forces is not required.** AI targets may include fielded

---

[1] Historical examples include: British air policing in the Middle East during the interwar period, French operations during the battle for Algeria, the US in Vietnam, the insurgent war in El Salvador, and recent US air operations in Iraq and Afghanistan.

[2] Not all air interdiction falls under the category of counterland. History has many examples of airpower interdicting the enemy's air or sea lines of communication; these are actually counterair or countersea missions even though they may have an interdiction effect at the operational level. Additionally, some interdiction missions may be considered a subset of strategic attack as described later in Chapter 1 in the section titled "Joint Integration and Complimentary Missions."

enemy forces or supporting components such as operational C2 nodes, communications networks, transportation systems, supply depots, military resources, and other vital infrastructure. When conducted as part of a joint campaign, interdiction needs the direction of a single commander who can exploit and coordinate all the forces involved, whether air-, space-, surface-, or information-based.

The combined force air and space component commander (CFACC) is normally the supported commander for the JFC's overall AI effort. When designated as the supported commander, the CFACC will conduct theater-wide or joint operating area (JOA)-wide AI in direct support of the JFC's overall theater objectives. With the preponderance of AI assets and the ability to plan, task, and control joint air operations, the CFACC can best plan and execute AI. The CFACC recommends theater and/or JOA-wide targeting priorities and, in coordination with other component commanders, forwards the air apportionment recommendation to the JFC. The CFACC, using the priorities or percentages established by the JFC's air apportionment decision, then plans and executes the theater and/or JOA-wide interdiction effort.

Close Air Support

CAS is air action by fixed- and rotary-winged aircraft against hostile targets that are in close proximity to friendly forces and which require detailed integration of each air mission with the fire and movement of those forces (see JP 3-09.3, *Joint Tactics, Techniques, and Procedures for Close Air Support*). CAS provides supporting firepower in offensive and defensive operations to destroy, disrupt, suppress, fix, harass, neutralize, or delay enemy targets as an element of joint fire support. The speed, range, and maneuverability of airpower allow CAS assets to attack targets that other supporting arms may not be able to engage effectively. CAS can be conducted at any place and time friendly forces are in close proximity to enemy forces and, at times, may be the best means to exploit tactical opportunities. Although in isolation it rarely achieves campaign-level objectives, at times it may be the more critical mission due to its contribution to campaign objectives. CAS should be planned to prepare the conditions for success or reinforce successful attacks of surface forces. CAS can halt attacks, help create breakthroughs, destroy targets of opportunity, cover retreats, and guard flanks. To be most effective, however, CAS should be used at decisive points in a battle and should normally be massed to apply concentrated combat power and saturate defenses. Equally important is that the appropriate level of C2, with appropriate release authority at a commensurate level, be in place to facilitate the expeditious application of airpower in rapidly changing scenarios. In fluid, high-intensity warfare, the need for terminal control, the unpredictability of the tactical situation, the risk of fratricide, and the proliferation of lethal ground-based air defenses make CAS especially challenging.

CAS requires a significant level of coordination between air and surface forces to produce desired effects. CAS employment should be safe, accurate, and timely to create effects that support the ground scheme of maneuver. The fluidity of the ground situation that exists within this close proximity usually requires real-time direction from a joint terminal attack controller to ensure that targets of highest priority to the ground commander are struck. Additionally, when friendly forces are within close proximity, more restrictive control measures may be required to integrate CAS with surface maneuver and joint fires. Integrating airpower and surface maneuver is an important factor for mitigating fratricide from both air-delivered weapons and surface fires. Thus, Airmen should consider two key factors when employing CAS: the need for flexible, real-time targeting guidance and the avoidance of hitting friendly ground forces in close proximity to the target.

Types of AI and CAS

Counterland missions are either scheduled or on-call. Scheduled missions result from preplanned requests during the normal air tasking order (ATO) cycle and allow for detailed coordination between the tactical air and ground units involved. Additionally, preplanned requests may result in counterland sorties in an on-call status (either airborne or ground alert) to cover periods of expected enemy action, respond to immediate requests, or attack dynamic targets. Scheduled AI missions use detailed intelligence to attack known or anticipated targets in an operational area to generate effects that achieve JFC objectives. Scheduled CAS missions are normally dedicated to a specific ground unit or operation. Air planners attach a "G" or "X" prefix to the ATO mission identifier to designate either ground or airborne alert, respectively.

- ✪ **GAI** is a mission placed on ground alert to provide responsive AI throughout the theater in response to emerging targets.

- ✪ **XAI** is a mission that pursues a designated area versus a particular target. XAI may fly airborne alert or search particular areas to strike at targets of opportunity.

- ✪ **GCAS** is a mission placed on ground alert status to provide responsive air support to ground forces that encounter substantial enemy resistance. CAS assets located close to the supported ground forces normally provide faster response times. GCAS missions may be changed to XCAS as the situation dictates.

- ✪ **XCAS** is a mission on airborne alert status in the vicinity of ground forces that expect to encounter enemy resistance. XCAS sorties typically remain in established holding patterns to provide responsive air support while awaiting tasking from any ground unit that needs CAS. If no tasking evolves during the vulnerability period, XCAS missions may swing to an AI role if other appropriate targets exist.

Some counterland missions may not clearly fall under the traditional definition of CAS and AI, but are still examples of airpower used against enemy surface forces or supporting infrastructure--the generic term "attack" may be used in such cases. Other labels such as strategic attack describe air-to-ground missions that fall under a different operational function than counterland.

> *Theater battle management core systems (TBMCS) has a myriad of "mission type" descriptors for missions ranging from direct support of surface forces, to the independent application of airpower supporting JFC objectives in the absence of surface forces. Mission type descriptors and their prefixes should not be confused with or tied to supported/supporting relationships. For example, an XAI mission using SOF as a sensor could quickly devolve to a CAS mission if the SOF unit were compromised. In this case, airpower supported by SOF becomes SOF supported by airpower very quickly, and is transparent to the TBMCS mission type planned.*

Scheduled AI missions can be dynamically retasked to provide CAS or attack time-sensitive targets if requisites such as aircrew qualifications, weapons load, and weapons fusing are compatible. Commanders and planners should carefully consider the resultant balance between effectiveness and efficiency caused by keeping a portion of air assets in reserve when apportioning ground-based and air alert missions.

Immediate requests usually result from situations that develop after the suspense for preplanned requests in a particular ATO cycle. Dynamic targeting provides a responsive use of on-call or dynamically retasked counterland missions to exploit enemy vulnerability that may be of limited duration. However, dynamic targeting may lead to an overall reduction in the probability of success because of reduced time for mission preparation and target study. Chapters 2 and 3 provide an expanded discussion of scheduled and on-call counterland missions.

Derivative Missions Associated with Counterland

Derivative mission-types are frequently tasked to complement and support counterland operations. The following discussion briefly describes the two most common missions that are associated with, and facilitate the effective accomplishment of, CAS and AI.

- ✪ **Forward Air Controller (Airborne) (FAC[A]).** FAC(A) missions provide joint terminal attack control for CAS aircraft operating in close proximity to friendly ground forces. Because of the risk of fratricide, FAC(A)s are specially trained aviation officers qualified to provide delivery clearance to CAS aircraft. The FAC(A) is the only person cleared to perform such control from the air, and can be especially useful in controlling CAS against targets that are beyond the visual range of friendly ground forces.

- ✪ **Strike Coordination and Reconnaissance (SCAR).** SCAR missions use aircraft to detect targets for dedicated AI missions in a specified geographic zone. The area may be defined by a box or grid where worthwhile potential targets are known or suspected to exist, or where mobile enemy surface units have relocated because of ground fighting.

SCAR missions are normally part of the C2 interface to coordinate multiple flights, detect targets, kill targets, neutralize enemy air defenses, and provide BDA. SCAR aircrew perform a similar function for AI missions that FAC(A) provide for CAS missions. Typical tasks include cycling multiple attacking flights through the target area and providing prioritized targeting guidance to maximize the effect of each sortie. Although fighter aircraft often accomplish SCAR missions, other platforms such as the Joint Surveillance Target Attack Radar System (JSTARS) and MQ-1/MQ-9 Predator UAS' can perform SCAR tasks such as locating, verifying, and cross cueing other assets to positively identify moving targets; procedurally controlling and sequencing aircraft; and passing target updates. The MQ-1 and MQ-9 can also find, fix, and track potential targets for subsequent AI missions. These platforms may also be able to engage targets on their own, buddy lase for manned aircraft, and provide BDA for the same mission. Optimally, the deconfliction and sequencing of aircraft is best performed by an E-3 airborne warning and control system (AWACS) or a ground-based control and reporting center (CRC).

Even though some SCAR responsibilities are similar to that of a FAC(A), *SCAR aircrew DO NOT have the authority to provide terminal attack control.* FAC(A)s undergo specialized training to effectively coordinate and integrate air-ground forces to conduct terminal attack control safely during CAS—a SCAR pilot does not have these specialized qualifications.

The bottom line: a FAC(A) can conduct SCAR but a SCAR aircrew cannot conduct FAC(A) duties. Planners and commanders need to understand this important nuance when tasking XAI missions or diverting airborne aircraft to an immediate CAS request (in addition to the fact that not all AI aircrews are qualified to conduct CAS).

JOINT CONSIDERATIONS

When discussing the use of air and space power in counterland operations, it is necessary to recognize the contribution of other components' aviation arms. Navy, Marine Corps, Army, and SOF assets can be used for both AI and CAS. While the primary task for Marine aviation is support to their own ground forces, excess Marine sorties may execute other elements of the JFC's plan. Scout and attack helicopters may also prove valuable platforms for counterland missions even though they lack the speed, range, and survivability of fixed-wing assets. Although the Army does not consider their helicopters CAS platforms, they can nevertheless employ CAS tactics, techniques, and procedures (TTP) when operating in support of land forces. Depending on circumstances and threat, SOF AC-130s may be available to support certain counterland operations. Air and surface-launched cruise missiles can also be employed for interdiction, as can the ATACMS. In multinational coalitions, air forces from allied nations will usually be available for counterland employment.

Regardless of which component the assets come from, the counterland effort is guided by a single air and space component commander and directly supports the overall joint campaign. Centralized control is a fundamental tenet that commanders must exercise to guarantee the concentration of air and space power where it is needed most. The CFACC is normally the supported commander for the JFC's overall AI effort. When designated as the supported commander, the CFACC will conduct theater-wide or JOA-wide AI in direct support of the JFC's overall theater objectives. This functional responsibility is executed by engaging the enemy across the theater wherever valuable AI targets are found, to include those found inside a surface area of operations (AO). AI used in this manner tends to have the greatest overall effect on the enemy, but the results may be delayed in comparison with AI employed closer to the ground battle. If theater objectives dictate, AI may operate in support of a particular portion of the theater where it is more closely integrated with the ground battle. This form of AI may strike targets nominated through the joint targeting process by either the air or surface component and often produces results visible to the surface commander more quickly than a theater-wide AI effort. These results also tend to be smaller in scope and shorter in duration. The most detailed integration of air and ground components is found in CAS where the air attack and ground battle are essentially a single cohesive operation. Proper integration of counterland and surface operations is vital to the success of both, and the synergistic effect of integrated operations is often much greater than the sum of individual air and surface operations. This will be especially true if a single, integrated joint operations plan is employed instead of attempting to synchronize individual plans developed by the various components.

The Airman's perception of depth differs from that of the Soldier, in that air and space power can reach to any depth of the battlespace—from the close battle area back to and beyond the enemy's heartland. As an aerial maneuver force, counterland operations forces should not be considered as "flying artillery." Counterland assets have much greater range and targeting options; can adapt to changing situations while en route to the target area; can retarget based on onboard or offboard information updates; can fight their way through enemy defenses; and can orbit over a given area while reconnoitering for targets of opportunity. Depending on the designated strategy, air and space power's reach enables a commander to focus counterland effects in a small area or disperse them uniformly across the theater at whatever depth is required. While in some instances it may be appropriate for the joint air component to be given responsibility for an AO, such as western Iraq during Operation IRAQI FREEDOM, it should not be limited to a single or even multiple independent AOs. Joint doctrine confirms this view by stating that AOs are defined by the JFC for land, maritime, and special operations forces for use by land, naval, and special operations component commanders (See JP 3-0, *Doctrine for Joint Operations*).

Air and surface maneuver forces share supporting roles during counterland operations. CAS represents aerial maneuver in direct support of surface maneuver. Air attack of ground-nominated AI targets is aerial maneuver indirectly supporting ground maneuver. Air attack against theater-wide AI targets is aerial maneuver that either provides general support to the ground force or directly achieves JFC objectives. Indeed, in some circumstances ground maneuver may support aerial maneuver by forcing the enemy into a position that is more vulnerable to air attack, enabling air and space power to deliver a vital blow. Moreover, SOF have proven extremely effective for target identification and cueing, as was the case during Operations ENDURING FREEDOM and IRAQI FREEDOM. In those unusual circumstances in which air and space forces conduct AI in the absence of friendly surface forces, enemy forces are able to disperse and seek cover in a way that complicates the problem for Airmen. However, as was shown in Operation ALLIED FORCE, air and space power can still create decisive effects and lead to success for the joint force. Whether air, space, or surface forces are the decisive element is not what matters. Instead, it is important to realize that the proper integration of air, space, and surface forces is required for successful joint operations.

Fires are "the effects of lethal or nonlethal weapons." Joint fires are "fires produced during the employment of forces from two or more components in coordinated action toward a common objective" (JP 1-02, *DOD Dictionary of Military and Associated Terms*). Counterland itself is not joint fires; rather, it represents a form of aerial maneuver, which delivers fires on various targets as required. Those counterland missions that are apportioned to support another component, such as CAS and some AI, can be defined as meeting the description of "two or more components in coordinated action." Therefore, the application of these missions can be called joint fires. Those missions that operate in direct support of theater strategy, such as theater-wide AI, are not operating in "coordinated action" with another component, rather they are conducting missions with organic forces in support of a scheme of maneuver. Therefore, the fires produced by those missions are not joint fires.

ELEMENTS OF EFFECTIVE COUNTERLAND OPERATIONS

Effective counterland operations share a number of common elements that lead to the attainment of operational objectives, such as destruction of enemy forces or infrastructure. To what degree each will contribute to the operation depends on such variables as the nature of the conflict, geographic location, weather, and characteristics of the enemy.

Air Control

Successful counterland operations require a certain degree of freedom to act without enemy interference. Providing both the freedom to attack and freedom from attack, **air superiority** is that degree of air advantage possessed by one force over another that permits the conduct of operations in the air domain at a given time and place without *prohibitive* interference by the opposing force. Air superiority over counterland operations allows combat aircraft to focus on target acquisition and weapons delivery parameters, thus increasing the chances of achieving desired effects.

Air supremacy is an additional degree of air control, where the opposing force is incapable of *effective* interference in the air domain. While this level of control is desirable in the air domain, it may not be required for successful counterland operations, and may be too costly in terms of asset apportionment. Assets dedicated to air supremacy may be used more wisely in support of land forces or other JFC objectives, if the level of interference by opposing air assets is acceptable or negligible.

While **air supremacy** relates to the air domain, **air dominance** is the highest level of air control that allows us to focus on affecting *surface* events. Air dominance does not require unopposed use of the air domain, but indicates a level or control in the air that allows us to apportion assets against surface objectives, reducing the ability of enemy forces to effectively employ on land or sea. In other words, air control describes our level of ascendancy in the air domain, while air dominance goes further to describe how we use that level of air control to affect enemy surface forces.

Although some aircraft are capable of self defense, gaining air superiority before conducting counterland operations will increase the chances of mission success without excessive losses. Stealth technology offers a means of minimizing much of the enemy air threat when air superiority is in dispute and may allow some counterland operations even in the face of heavy enemy air defenses. Multi-role fighters have significant air-to-air capabilities that can serve as a defense against enemy air threats even while carrying a full load of air-to-ground weapons. However, whether stealth or self-escorted fighter, attack assets are likely to be prioritized against counterair targets until air superiority is achieved.

The risk of conducting counterland operations prior to achieving air superiority must be balanced with the threat posed by the enemy air and surface forces. Counterland operations conducted prior to achieving air superiority should normally be reserved for those targets that represent immediate and critical danger.

Joint Integration and Complementary Operations

Counterland operations are most effective when planned and conducted synergistically with other air, land, sea, space, and special operations forces. AI can create opportunities for commanders to exploit, and centralized joint planning ensures the optimum employment of AI. AI levies requirements on air planners and combined air and space operations center (CAOC) personnel to plan, execute, and assess AI in coordination with surface components, when appropriate. Air and surface commanders need to work together to: 1) identify crucial targets; 2) decide when, where, and how to attack them; and 3) determine how surface operations and AI can best complement each other to achieve JFC objectives and to create opportunities for other maneuver elements to exploit. The integration of several other air and space power functions can significantly contribute to the effectiveness of counterland operations.

- ✪ **Counterair** operations enable the effective execution of counterland operations by suppressing or eliminating surface-to-air and air-to-air threats. Though it is possible to conduct counterland operations without control of the air, such operations would likely be both costly and ineffective.

- ✪ **Strategic Attack** and counterland operations complement one another through their synergistic effects. Strategic attack operations directly target enemy centers of gravity such as leadership, conflict-sustaining resources, and/or strategy. Targets may include strategic C2 nodes, munitions plants, heavy industry, energy production, or weapons of mass destruction (WMD). Thus, in one sense, strategic attack disrupts or destroys such targets at the source, while counterland operations normally target operational fielded forces and their supporting infrastructure in the field.

Strategic interdiction is a label often used for those strategic attack operations that seek to cut off the flow of strategic resources or other material vital to the adversary's war effort. This type of interdiction differs from the more familiar counterland AI in that enemy fielded forces or their supporting infrastructure are not directly involved. A good example of strategic interdiction was the effort by US submarines, joined later by US Army Air Force bombers and fighters, against Japanese merchant shipping during World War II.

- ✪ **Space Force Enhancement** multiplies the effectiveness and increases the lethality of counterland forces through five force enhancement functions: intelligence, surveillance, and reconnaissance; integrated tactical warning and attack assessment; environmental monitoring; communications; and positioning, navigation, and timing. ISR provides location and disposition of adversary assets as well as tactical BDA. Environmental monitoring provides meteorological data as well as imagery of surface conditions, vegetation and land use. Communications allows counterland forces the means to disseminate plans, orders and force status over long distances, and provides critical connectivity for maneuver forces operating beyond inherent communication networks. Finally, the global positioning system (GPS) constellation allows precise, reliable blue force tracking, navigation of forces, combat identification, and target weaponeering for precision munitions.

- ✪ **Intelligence, Surveillance, and Reconnaissance** serves a vital role in the planning and prosecution of counterland operations. Persistent, accurate, and timely intelligence aids commanders in anticipating environmental factors, predicting enemy actions, identifying counterland targets, and combat assessment.

- ✪ **Information Operations (IO)** targeted against enemy information systems can have collateral effects on the entire enemy system through the disruption, degradation, denial, and destruction of its C2 networks. Effective IO can deceive the enemy and assist friendly forces to seize the initiative. Additionally, the synergistic effects of psychological operations (PSYOP) conducted in parallel with counterland operations combine to give the air component a pivotal role in achieving the overall goals of any joint campaign. The psychological shock of massed air attack and information operations can be overwhelming to the enemy's fielded forces, especially when those forces have already been strained by surface combat. Public affairs (PA) also play a role in IO. Effective employment of PA operations keeps global audiences aware of the precision and effectiveness of counterland operations via the news media. PA operations are the first line of defense against enemy efforts to leverage collateral damage or fratricide events for propaganda purposes.

- ✪ **Special Operations Forces (SOF)** complement and support conventional counterland operations by providing intelligence, target cueing, terminal attack control, guidance for precision-guided munitions (PGMs), and post attack assessment. SOF may also employ organic weapons systems such as fixed or rotary-winged gunships, and special operations ground teams.

⊙ **Weather Services** provide timely, accurate, and relevant environmental information essential to the effective planning and execution of air, ground, and space operations. Weather information influences the timing of force employment as well as the selection of targets, routes, weapon systems and delivery tactics.

Appropriate Munitions, Assets, and Allocation

Proper munitions planning and employment are important factors for effective counterland operations. Numbers and types of munitions available, as well as those in the logistics pipeline, need to support specific requirements for a particular conflict. The munitions mix must correspond to the selected targeting strategy. Weapons loads and fuse settings should be tailored to the desired level of target destruction, neutralization, or suppression. Although precision munitions have become a primary weapon of choice, planners should realize that general-purpose bombs and cluster munitions may provide better effects in some situations. Planners should also consider the possibility of adverse weapons effects against friendly forces, such as the employment of time-delayed munitions against an enemy near advancing friendly forces. Precision munitions are uniquely valuable in attacking hardened point targets or for minimizing collateral damage. These highly accurate direct attack munitions provide rapid strike capability with maximum flexibility, while standoff precision weapons allow delivery platforms to remain outside the most heavily defended areas with nearly the same accuracies. Precision attack of key infrastructure, transportation, and C2 targets can cripple an enemy force's ability to maneuver, and has usually been the preferred use of limited PGM assets rather than attacking the enemy one vehicle at a time. However, with increased stockpiles, PGMs and inertially-aided munitions (IAMs) are particularly useful against a mechanized enemy force that places most of its combat power in various types of vehicles. If the number of precision munitions and aircraft available is high enough, counterland operations can inflict devastating losses on a mechanized enemy force through the simple expedient of vehicle-by-vehicle destruction. However, such a strategy of attrition must be considered in terms of both number of weapons required and the possible existence of more lucrative target sets and the time required to destroy enough of the enemy force to be operationally effective.

The CFACC's ability to conduct counterland operations successfully depends on the available type and quantity of air and space assets. Precision weapons delivery, stealth characteristics, and destructive power, combined with the inherent capability of the air and space component to mass effects against a given objective, can provide a substitute for raw numbers. The principles of mass and economy of force should be followed to ensure that adequate force is available to achieve the desired effects. Though many platforms can employ in the AI and CAS roles, some are better suited for each mission from both a training and equipment standpoint. In addition, it is important to understand that some units employing air-to-ground ordnance are not qualified for CAS, which has specific training and currency requirements. Commanders should carefully assess the desired munitions effects, aircrew training, and asset capabilities in light of the potential for fratricide.

Commanders should also understand the impact that AI/CAS allocation has on sortie throughput to increase counterland efficiency. During high-intensity operations, effective integration between air and land components increases tempo and efficiency. Because CAS requires detailed integration, the communications and procedures are much more involved than AI. Therefore, CAS execution tends to require more time, resources, and trained personnel. Because of these factors, C2 agencies can control significantly more AI sorties than CAS sorties per ATO cycle. When possible, air and ground commanders should synchronize their schemes of maneuver to minimize the area of detailed integration. That way, when JFC objectives call for the rapid destruction of enemy land forces, more airpower can be used against counterland targets when detailed integration is not necessary. This does not imply that the Air Force should divert its assets and abandon ground

Night attack capability for counterland has progressed from the flares used in World War II and the Korean War to modern infrared systems such as the low-altitude navigation and targeting infrared for night (LANTIRN) pods on this F-15E Strike Eagle. Improving technology has removed some of the night/adverse weather interdiction sanctuary formerly exploited by enemy surface forces.

forces. It simply means the air and ground components should coordinate their actions to maximize combat power throughout the battlefield.

Favorable Environmental Factors

Some argue that recent technologies have eliminated the sanctuaries of adverse weather and darkness. In some respects, this is true. The adverse effects of weather can be reduced through a combination of IAMs and on-board sensors that do not require optical guidance. GPS-assisted joint direct attack munitions (JDAM) and radar sensors can aid the weapons delivery process in conditions of poor visibility. During night operations, modern air-to-ground infrared (IR) systems often see better in darkness than in daylight, and night can make many enemy air defense systems less effective against counterland aircraft (especially attack helicopters which are typically limited to low altitude operations).

Despite technological advancements, poor environmental conditions can still negatively affect counterland operations. Some forms of adverse weather can interfere with the ability of airpower assets to reach the intended target while often hindering both detection and attack geometry. Many precision-guided weapons still rely on line of sight to the target for employment; conditions such as fog, low clouds, or battlefield obscuration can prevent visual contact and disrupt weapons delivery. Target identification is a critical factor when employing weapons in close proximity to ground forces.

Favorable weather is important to effective CAS, perhaps more so than other forms of air attack. Since identification of the target through visual or electro-optical means is usually required for target confirmation and fratricide avoidance, a low cloud deck can often prevent CAS missions from hitting their targets. Non-visual weapons deliveries using radar, GPS, or IAMs may allow CAS aircraft to hit stationary targets through the weather, but target coordinate accuracy will have to be confirmed to both the air and ground component's satisfaction before this option is used. This is especially important when assessing the risk of fratricide. The ground commander authorizes the attack and accepts responsibility of risk to friendly forces while the CFACC determines the minimum acceptable weather for CAS. In the absence of Air Force weather personnel, the air liaison officer (ALO) should advise the ground commander on what impact adverse weather will have on CAS. Although advanced navigation systems and targeting sensors lessen the consequences of adverse environmental conditions, technology will never completely alleviate the risk of fratricide or collateral damage. Individual controllers and aircrew must make the final call during mission execution if existing weather is above or below their mission minimums.

Environmental factors also affect surface forces. The rate and extent of enemy surface maneuver influenced by weather conditions may provide increased AI opportunities (for example, when enemy maneuver is restricted to a few major routes by seasonal conditions, it results in concentrated forces which are more easily destroyed or disrupted). Planners should use information from C2 systems or weather personnel to help gauge the effect of weather and environmental conditions on counterland operations.

SUMMARY

Counterland can play a key role in the successful outcome of a campaign or major operation across the range of military operations. Counterland operations require close integration with the JFC's overall strategy to be effective and must be tailored to the situation. Counterland may achieve tactical, operational, or strategic level effects. Counterland can complement, support, be supported by, or act independently of other joint force operations. Because air and space assets are a limited resource, joint counterland operations require unity of effort to achieve the desired synergy to achieve JFC objectives.

CHAPTER TWO

AIR INTERDICTION

GENESIS OF COUNTERLAND DOCTRINE

In theory and in practice, air support aircraft in 1918 had two categories of targets: objectives along the enemy's heavily defended frontal positions, which some generals called the "crust," and a whole range of targets extending twenty miles and more behind that crust. By the end of the war, a considerable body of opinion held that the chief contribution of aircraft should be against those objectives behind that crust. Enemy reinforcements moving up in column were much more visible and much more vulnerable than front-line troops in field fortifications, and there was less danger of confusing them with friendly ground forces. Then too, objectives behind the front lines tended to be less fiercely defended—no minor consideration, given the losses suffered by ground attack units. Additionally, excellent targets often lay beyond the effective range of friendly artillery, in a zone where only the airplane could reach them. Toward the end of the war, targets such as dense troop columns and convoys of vehicles appeared in great numbers.

—Lee Kennett,
Case Studies in the Development of Close Air Support

World War I pursuits like this SPAD XIII were often used for both "trench strafing" and "ground strafing" missions, which would today be categorized as close air support and air interdiction.

> *The disruption of hostile lines of communication (and at times lines of signal communication), the destruction of supply dumps, installations, and the attack on hostile troop concentrations in rear areas will cause the enemy great damage and may decide the battle.*
>
> **— US Army Field Manual 100-20,**
> ***Command and Employment of Air Power, 1943***

DEFINITION

AI is an air operation conducted to divert, disrupt, delay, or destroy the enemy's military potential before it can be brought to bear effectively against friendly forces, or to otherwise achieve JFC objectives. AI is conducted at such distance from friendly forces that detailed integration of each air mission with the fire and movement of friendly forces is not required. AI can significantly affect the overall course of a campaign. It contributes by disrupting the enemy's ability to command, mass, maneuver, withdraw, supply, and reinforce available combat power and by weakening the enemy physically and psychologically. AI creates opportunities for friendly commanders to exploit.

AI increases air and space power's efficiency because it does not require detailed integration with friendly forces. Detailed integration requires extensive communications, comprehensive deconfliction procedures, and meticulous planning. AI is inherently simpler to execute in this regard. Therefore, if the enemy surface force presents a lucrative target, AI conducted before friendly land forces make contact can significantly degrade the enemy's fighting ability and limit the need for CAS when the two forces meet in close combat.

The joint air component often conducts theater-wide air attacks against enemy land forces and their resources to achieve JFC objectives. This autonomous use of AI usually occurs outside of a surface component's AO. SOF air and ground assets may play a significant supporting role during AI with their ability to seamlessly integrate into the F2T2EA process. Operations DESERT STORM, ENDURING FREEDOM, and IRAQI FREEDOM are just a few modern examples where AI independently achieved JFC objectives through the direct attack of enemy land forces.

Using JFC priorities and understanding the land component's scheme of maneuver, the CFACC can employ AI to provide effects that facilitate and support the maneuver. The CFACC may support a land scheme of maneuver by conducting AI within a surface commander's AO. After coordinating priorities, effects, timing, and targets with surface components, the CFACC directs responsive AI across the JOA against enemy military capabilities that contribute directly to, or are maneuvering to reinforce, the conflict. US surface commanders often consider AI synonymous with what they express as "shaping" operations. From an Airman's perspective, shaping may be regarded as preparing the battlefield with AI to assist the land component's scheme of maneuver.

Air Interdiction vs. Shaping Operations

From a Soldier's perspective, shaping operations support the decisive operation by affecting enemy capabilities and forces, or by influencing enemy decisions. Shaping operations use all elements of combat power to neutralize or reduce enemy capabilities. (US Army Field Manual 3-0, Operations) As a result, Soldiers may consider AI as shaping which solely supports their maneuver elements. From an Airman's perspective, AI may be conducted either in support of surface force objectives or in direct support of JFC objectives; in the latter case, the air component commander might be the supported commander. Because of these slightly differing views, there is a potential for friction between the air and land components regarding supporting/supported roles and responsibility for planning. These situations require careful and continuing dialogue between the competing senior commanders and their common superior commander.

INTERDICTION OBJECTIVES

The desired objectives of AI are to divert, disrupt, delay, or destroy the enemy. It is not necessary for an AI operation to focus solely on a single objective; in fact, AI typically inflicts multiple effects on the enemy. The enemy army traveling to the front while under air attack will suffer some level of destruction. The remaining force will likely be delayed in getting to its destination and will suffer some level of physical and psychological disruption.

Divert

AI can divert enemy fielded forces from areas where they are critically needed. It may divert enemy ground forces to a location more favorable to the JFC and can also divert enemy naval, engineering, and personnel resources to the tasks of repairing and recovering damaged equipment and facilities as well as keeping lines of communication (LOCs) open. These diversions prevent enemy ground forces and their backup support resources from being employed for their intended purpose. Diversions can also cause circuitous routing along LOCs, resulting in additional delays for the enemy.

Disrupt

AI can disrupt the enemy's C2 systems, intelligence collection capability, transportation systems, supply lines, and psychological will. Disruption of enemy surface forces can be accomplished in a number of ways. A key part of the interdiction planner's task is to analyze the enemy army for critical vulnerabilities that, if attacked, will have a disruptive effect across significant portions of the enemy force. The presence of such targets, and the ability to attack them, will often determine whether disruption or destruction will be the primary effect mechanism planned for AI effort. This can include traditional supply targets such as ammunition or petroleum, oil, and lubricants (POL); LOCs used to transport the enemy force into combat; C2 systems that the enemy army requires to fight effectively; or anything else the enemy force depends on for success in combat. In analyzing the enemy, considerations include what reserves or workarounds the enemy has available, what time delay can be afforded before the effects must affect the enemy, what strategy the enemy is expected to employ, and what the actual battlefield situation is. Another way to neutralize the enemy surface force is to affect the morale of its troops, which has historically been a strongpoint of using airpower. Psychological uncertainty as to whether or not forces, materiel, or supplies will arrive can directly affect enemy commanders, their staffs, and forces.

Delay

AI can delay enemy forces and supplies. If part of the enemy surface force is destroyed, the enemy's efforts to avoid having the rest of its force suffer the same fate will often result in long delays or an outright halt to their movement to contact. When AI delays the enemy, friendly forces gain time. What JFCs do to improve their situation in the time gained is critical to any assessment of interdiction's contribution. However, an AI plan that focuses on delay does not guarantee a major impact on combat operations. In order for delay to have a major impact, either the enemy must face urgent movement requirements in support of its own operations or to counter friendly maneuver, or the delay must enhance the effect of planned friendly maneuver. It is advantageous for friendly forces to pressure their opponent to attempt urgent movement. Ideally, if the air component maintains the initiative, the opponent is forced to make unplanned urgent movements at times and places that maximize their exposure to AI. Delay is critical in achieving additional AI payoffs. For example, it can lengthen the time during which enemy land or naval forces are at risk of attack. When vehicles amass behind a damaged route segment, or ships are trapped in a harbor because of mines, a more concentrated set of targets and a longer period of exposure results. This makes the enemy easier to destroy or renders it ineffective.

Destroy

Destruction of the enemy surface force, supporting elements, and supplies is the most direct of the four objectives of AI. The enemy's perception of its imminent destruction can be as effective in achieving AI objectives as physically destroying target systems, if it causes the enemy to react in a way upon which friendly forces can capitalize. Destroying transportation systems is usually not an end in itself, but contributes to the delay, diversion, and disruption of enemy forces and materiel. The demonstrated or perceived ability to destroy may, by itself, achieve substantial delay and diversion of enemy resources. It may cause the enemy to move only at night or to mass air defense assets (which may be useful elsewhere) around critical transportation nodes. The enemy may have to divert engineering resources from other tasks to prepare alternate routes in anticipation of possible attacks. This may be true when transportation systems remain largely undamaged. However, destruction may also inhibit friendly freedom of action. For example, destruction of key transportation targets could hinder future surface operations that intend to use the same infrastructure. Appropriate coordination of AI with other joint force components helps preserve friendly freedom of action.

EFFECTS OF AIR INTERDICTION

AI effects differ with every situation and can significantly affect the course of a campaign or operation. Results against an enemy with minimal logistics requirements, a simple force structure, and primitive logistics systems differ from AI conducted against a highly mechanized, modern force possessing intensive logistics requirements. Interdiction conducted against enemy forces and logistics, without regard to the overall theater situation, may be largely ineffective; thus planning for interdiction should be closely integrated in the JFC's overall planning process.

The effectiveness of AI is largely dependent on a number of variables. The time required for AI to affect the enemy, and the duration and depth of those effects, depends on several factors. These factors include, but are not limited to, the distance between interdiction operations and the location of intended effects; the means and rate of enemy movement (ships, trains, aircraft, trucks); the physical target (forces, supplies, fuel, munitions, infrastructure); the level of enemy activity; enemy tactics; and the resilience of the targeted force or system. For example, AI will have a more robust effect in linear combat against a modern, mobile, conventional force using significant resources. Moreover, the timing and magnitude of effects will vary depending on where AI is conducted and the nature of the enemy. On one hand, AI deep in the battlespace will usually produce extensive, protracted effects that take longer to occur. On the other hand, AI close to the front lines typically produces immediate, but geographically limited, effects. Thus, during major operations and campaigns, AI effects are typically more apparent by influencing an enemy's ability to command, mass, maneuver, supply, and reinforce available conventional combat forces. When conducted during stability operations, AI may have negligible effects against an insurrection that employs a shadowy force structure, a simple logistics net, and unconventional tactics. However, with timely, accurate intelligence and persistent operations, AI can disrupt enemy supply operations, destroy weapons caches, or deny sanctuary to insurgents. To maximize AI's potential, commanders must understand how its effects will differ depending on the nature of the conflict being fought.

Whether the Air Force is involved in major operations and campaigns or smaller scale contingencies, **AI can channel movements, constrict logistics systems, disrupt communications, force urgent movement, and attrit enemy fielded forces.**

Disruptive Counterland Operations During DESERT STORM

Even Iraqis who had foreseen heavy air attacks commented that the Coalition bombing was more continuous, devastating, and wide-scale than what they had expected. The round-the-clock bombing experienced by some units during portions of the air campaign proved particularly stressful for both officers and enlisted personnel because it deprived them of sleep and allowed them little opportunity to perform their duties. One senior officer reported that he could rarely sleep more than two hours at a time and that the constant pounding shattered the soldiers' nerves, causing some men, as he put it, nearly to go mad. The bombing produced this strong psychological effect even though it caused the Iraqi officer's division relatively light casualties: perhaps 100 men killed and another 150 wounded.

The magnitude of the B-52 bomb loads had a tremendous psychological effect on the Iraqi troops. Even though few Iraqi POWs or line crossers reported that their units were actually hit in B-52 strikes, many had seen B-52s attacking other units in the distance and had felt the ground tremors from B-52 bomb detonations. The sound and vibrations of the B-52 detonations—even when the actual strike zone was as far away as 40 kilometers—spawned suspense and fear because the soldiers imagined that they would be the next target of attack, and they realized that their bunkers were neither sufficiently deep nor sufficiently hard to protect them.

An Iraqi officer told his interrogator that he had surrendered because of B-52 strikes. "But your position was never attacked by B-52s," his interrogator exclaimed. "That is true," the Iraqi officer replied, "but I saw one that had been attacked."

—Stephen T. Hosmer,
Psychological Effects of US Air Operations in Four Wars: 1941-1991

Channeling Enemy Movements

AI channels the movement of ground forces when conditions force the enemy to maneuver through or along predictable avenues. This generally results from the lack of transportation routes, manmade and natural obstacles, and other geographic constraints. The fewer the routes available to transport enemy supplies and reinforcements, the greater the loss or delay caused by severing those routes. Attacks on enemy lateral LOCs can channel movement, impair reinforcement, reduce operational cohesion, and create conditions for defeating the enemy in detail. Geography influences the rate of enemy movement, the size of the force to be moved, where it can move, and the means required to move the force. Geography may also restrict or channel ground movement, creating chokepoints and concentrated targets. In cases where geography favors rapid movement of enemy forces, AI assets can create artificial or temporary chokepoints by laying large numbers of scatterable mines, dropping bridges, or collapsing tunnels.

Air component planners must coordinate the AI effort with the land component's overall scheme of maneuver. LOCs used by the enemy may also facilitate rapid advance of our own ground forces, requiring properly coordinated trade-offs between interdicting the enemy and preserving key routes for advancing friendly ground units.

Constricting the Enemy's Logistics System

Heavy ground combat creates demands on enemy fielded forces and speeds consumption of vital war materiel. This in turn increases the effects of AI operations by straining the enemy support system and reducing stockpiles. For surface combat to take place, soldiers and their weapons, ammunition, food, fuel, and communications must get to the battle. When the enemy consumes large quantities of supplies because of heavy combat or extensive movement, interdiction operations have an accelerated impact for two reasons. First, when opponents are under heavy pressure, they may be forced to use up stockpiles reserved for ongoing or future operations. Inability to stockpile supplies makes it more difficult for the enemy to initiate large-scale offensive operations. Second, high consumption drives an enemy to use more direct routes, making them more vulnerable to interdiction attacks. The nature of ground combat also determines which supporting elements are most critical at any given time, as which items of supply and infrastructure are critical can vary greatly with the situation. Historically, an enemy army fighting under static conditions is more affected by the destruction of munitions, while a highly mobile enemy is more disrupted by the loss of fuel and transportation.

The less surplus capacity the enemy's logistics system has, the less it can compensate for damage. Degrading the mobility of the enemy's distribution system hinders its ability to redistribute assets to effectively counter friendly operations. When attacking the enemy's logistic systems, it is normally prudent to concentrate efforts on a small number of limiting factors such as concentrations of supplies; petroleum, oils, and lubricants; storage and resupply systems; or soft vehicles. There may not be enough interdiction assets to attack all of an enemy's logistic systems, even sequentially over time.

The enemy transportation system itself must also be broken down into components when analyzing for weaknesses to attack. Most transportation systems consist of the actual conduit for travel (roads, rail, etc.), vehicles used to transport troops or supplies along the conduit, energy required for those vehicles to operate (typically POL or electricity), C2 to run the transportation system, and repair facilities to keep the system operating. The loading and unloading points in the transportation system may prove especially lucrative, as large concentrations of enemy forces or supplies are often found there. Examples include rail yards, harbors, and airfields. If forces or supplies are critically needed at the front, the enemy may not have the luxury of dispersing them during loading or unloading, which increases vulnerability to attack. Moreover, environmental impacts on the transportation system can create additional chokepoints worth exploiting. In many cases, the enemy will use the same transportation system for both forces and supplies. Under such circumstances, destroying or degrading the enemy's LOCs will affect both their force mobility and resupply capability. When analyzing an enemy transportation network for importance to their overall strategy, all possible uses for such a system must be considered. Before making the decision to interdict the enemy's transportation network, it must be analyzed for surplus capacity and reconstitution capability. Failure to do this has sometimes led to large-scale AI efforts that had little real chance of success (e.g., the limited effectiveness in halting activity on the Ho Chi Minh Trail during the Vietnam War).

Disrupting Enemy Communications

The enemy's combat operations may be disrupted with attacks on their C2 nodes; the level of C2 disruption must be commensurate with overall objectives. C2 attacks may seek complete isolation of enemy combat forces from higher headquarters, or such attacks may force the enemy to use less capable, less secure backup communication systems that can be more easily exploited by friendly forces. When the enemy employs a rigid, top-down C2 doctrine, they can be particularly vulnerable to the disruptive effects of C2 interdiction. This is especially true when the enemy has not had a long preparation period to exercise their plan, or when the conflict has moved beyond the initial stages. Conversely, an enemy that practices a high degree of C2 autonomy will likely be less affected by attacks on their C2 network. When the ground situation has been static for long periods before the campaign, chances are greater that the enemy has planned and trained for either offensive or defensive operations. Under such circumstances, attacks on enemy C2 are less likely to have significant effects, as the enemy is still able to react in a scripted manner. Once enough time has elapsed for events to overcome a preplanned enemy response, attacks on C2 will impair their ability to respond and pay larger dividends on the battlefield. In some circumstances, such as when the operations plan includes forcing the enemy to react to friendly maneuver, complete destruction of their C2 architecture would be counterproductive. The capability to affect the enemy through nonlethal information operations must also be considered, as this approach may lead to better overall results while freeing up conventional attack assets for other forms of AI.

Forcing Urgent Movement Upon the Enemy

The enemy may execute urgent movement for several reasons: an attempt to achieve surprise, the need to attack before reinforcements or supplies arrive, the requirement for rapid reinforcement of threatened defensive positions, the attempt to exploit offensive operations, or when driven to urgent movement by interdiction effects. Under these conditions, the enemy has a strong incentive to attain specific objectives within time constraints. Rapid movement of enemy forces and supplies may make them more vulnerable to AI. They generally become more concentrated while traversing more exposed and predictable avenues, foregoing time-consuming camouflage and concealment efforts. However, urgent movements are temporary due to a desire to limit exposure. For friendly forces to capitalize on such opportunities, we must deny the enemy mobility when they need it most. Close coordination is required among all forces to take full advantage of the situation. Additionally, commanders require access to information systems able to process real-time and near real-time intelligence in order to exploit the capabilities of interdiction and opportunities that AI operations create. Friendly forces must take full advantage of all reconnaissance and surveillance assets, from air- and space-borne sensors to SOF air and ground elements, to detect when these movements occur. Coordination is required among all forces to take full advantage of the situation in the time provided; otherwise, the enemy may escape the desired effects of AI.

Attrition of the Enemy

AI can attrit enemy forces and materiel, tipping the balance of forces in favor of friendly units. AI against enemy fielded forces has traditionally been more limited than the other effects, mainly due to the difficulty of finding and targeting individual guns or vehicles. Although modern sensor and weapons technology enables us to more accurately engage enemy targets, commanders must not be lulled into the belief that this will assure the direct destruction of enemy forces. Resources, terrain, weather, enemy actions, and enemy characteristics are just a few variables to consider when developing an AI strategy.

The fact that directly attacking individual enemy forces is possible does not mean that it is always the most efficient approach in terms of munitions and sorties available. Although the direct destruction of individual enemy forces has an immediate impact on enemy combat power, it usually requires more assets due to the larger number of individual targets—especially if they are dispersed or dug in. Often, the isolation of large enemy formations by destroying enemy logistics nets, sustaining resources, and supporting infrastructure can achieve more widespread results than attacking individual tanks or artillery pieces.

Terrain and weather affect the ability to attrit enemy forces. Attacking an enemy in open terrain in good weather significantly differs from striking an enemy in rough wooded terrain under a layer of adverse weather. As an example, exposed Iraqi forces were much easier AI targets for coalition airpower during Operation DESERT STORM than dispersed Serbian forces that took cover using trees, valleys, and adverse weather conditions during Operation ALLIED FORCE.

Enemy characteristics influence an attrition-based strategy. The number and vulnerability of enemy fielded force components, along with the enemy's ability to replace its losses, must be weighed against the expected results of targeting the supporting infrastructure. An attrition-based strategy against enemy fielded forces tends to produce intense localized results with fewer disruptive effects across the entire enemy system. Psychologically disruptive effects, however, may prove to be an added benefit. Enemy movement also influences the ability to destroy enemy fielded forces. During DESERT STORM and IRAQI FREEDOM, the presence of coalition land forces forced the enemy to react *en masse,* leaving them detectable and exposed to air attack. However, because Operation ALLIED FORCE saw no use of significant coalition land forces, the Serbs were able to use dispersion, deception, and concealment tactics. Thus, friendly ground maneuver that forces an enemy to react and become predictable can make an attrition strategy viable and more effective. Retreating enemy forces remain a legitimate target in AI operations as such forces may be available for continual use by the opposing commander. However, surrendering (or surrendered) forces are not legitimate targets, if it has been established that such forces are surrendering, and the attacking force is in a position to know of the surrender.

TYPES OF AIR INTERDICTION REQUESTS

AI requests fall into two categories: preplanned and immediate. Each type of request is influenced by a variety of factors. Unless time constraints dictate otherwise, preplanned requests should always be accomplished to allow for proper weapon-target combination, target area tactics planning, threat avoidance, weather study, and other variables, to maximize the probability of target destruction with minimum losses. Attacking mobile or short-notice targets provides a more flexible response that can capitalize on opportunities, but lack of mission planning can reduce effectiveness and higher friendly losses may be expected. Real-time information technology and digital cockpit imagery reduces, but does not eliminate, this factor.

Preplanned Requests

Preplanned AI is the normal method of operation in which aircraft attack prearranged or planned targets. This mode is used to hit specific targets that are known in advance, and detailed intelligence information is available to support strike planning. Preplanned attacks are normally flown against fixed targets or against mobile targets that are not expected to move in the interval between planning and execution (e.g., revetted tanks). Target information for scheduled AI can come from sources that vary from overhead reconnaissance to ground-based SOF. Preplanned AI is conducted within the normal air tasking cycle and provides enough time for close coordination with other joint force components. It is crucial for component liaisons to communicate and work together to facilitate centralized planning and effective integration, and avoid duplicating effort. Preplanned AI requests evolve into scheduled and on-call missions.

- ✪ **Scheduled missions** are planned against targets on which air attacks are delivered at a specific time.

- ✪ **On-call missions** are planned against targets other than scheduled missions for which a need can be anticipated but which will be delivered upon request rather than a specific time.

On-call AI missions can produce responsive, flexible effects. In cases where a specific area to search for enemy AI targets cannot be predetermined, these missions are designated as XAI or GAI on the ATO and may be put on an airborne alert status. The appropriate C2 agency provides guidance to a specific target, kill box, or target area. XAI missions will normally be given a target priority list or other guidance defining which targets to attack for greatest disruption of the enemy. This set of target priorities may be available prior to takeoff, or may be passed in flight by an appropriate C2 agency such as a forward air controller (FAC), a SCAR, an air support operations center (ASOC), an AWACS, or an E-8 JSTARS. If no targets are discovered in the designated area, XAI missions should be prepared to proceed to a backup target if available or requested by the designated controlling agency. Planners should attempt to match proper weapons loads with expected target types to maximize XAI effects. When flexible AI is flown in direct support of the surface component, the target priorities should reflect those established by the surface component and communicated via the appropriate component liaison officer (LNO) within the theater air-ground system (TAGS). The ASOC normally coordinates and directs preplanned AI requests flown short of the fire support coordination line (FSCL).

Immediate Requests

Immediate AI meets specific requests which arise during the course of a battle and which by their sudden nature are not planned in accordance with the normal ATO process. Immediate AI requests can respond to unplanned or unanticipated targets that require urgent, time-critical attention. It should be noted that many immediate requests for AI allow sufficient time for in-depth planning prior to execution even if those requests fall inside of the normal 72-hour air tasking cycle that defines "immediate." Immediate AI often responds to attack requests against dynamic and time-sensitive targets.

Dynamic targeting. Dynamic targeting is the active process of identifying, prosecuting, and effectively engaging emerging targets. The primary focus of dynamic targeting should be the prosecution of JFC designated and prioritized time-sensitive targets (TST) and functional component-critical targets. The destruction of these priority targets is considered critical for achieving JFC objectives and thus requires the establishment of detailed decision and authorization guidance for each designated target type to ensure rapid and effective engagement. It is important to limit the total number of TST class designations to only those meeting the definition of JP 1-02 and to provide to all levels of C2 and force application clear guidance on what constitutes a TST/component-critical target to avoid diversion of assets from the JFC's overall plan.

Time-sensitive targets. The CFACC may recommend TSTs to the JFC. TSTs are those targets of such high priority that the JFC designates them as requiring immediate response because they pose (or will soon pose) a clear and present danger to friendly forces or are highly lucrative, fleeting targets of opportunity (JP 1-02). TSTs are prosecuted using the dynamic targeting process above, but are of higher priority and may require additional coordination with other components and/or the joint task force. The destruction of these high payoff targets is considered critical for achieving JFC objectives. The JFC is ultimately responsible for TST prosecution and relies on the component commanders for conducting TST operations.

When using on-call or dynamically re-tasked assets, immediate AI often relies on an offboard sensor such as JSTARS to provide initial target detection and attack targeting information. Using real-time target information via data-link, response times can be as short as a few minutes, depending on the distances and C2 arrangements involved. Immediate AI requests allow airborne assets to exploit enemy vulnerability that may be of limited duration. It can work particularly well when attacking enemy ground forces on the move in the enemy rear area and provide a responsive use of counterland attack when supporting the ground component. The ASOC normally coordinates and directs immediate AI requests flown short of the FSCL.

The same quick-responsive nature of immediate AI that allows it to take advantage of fleeting opportunities can also have a negative impact on individual mission success. Scheduled missions allow aircrews more time to study the target imagery and to align attack axes to optimize weapons effects. Detailed study can reduce threat exposure and allow mission planners to optimize the weapon's fusing for maximum effect. Preplanning allows better packaging of strike and support assets when required. The bottom line for dynamic targeting of airborne assets is that it should be used in those cases when the need for a short reaction time outweighs the reduced effectiveness that may result when compared with preplanned operations. Moreover, opportunity costs must be considered. Commanders should ensure the benefits of diverting air and space power away from a preplanned target outweigh the costs by pondering several variables. *Is it affordable to delay striking a preplanned target? What are the priorities? Will diverting airpower to an unplanned target create greater effects or is it less efficient?* In short, the payoff of striking a dynamic target should be worth the cost of diverting preplanned assets.

To increase battlespace awareness during dynamic targeting, C2 elements must ensure that aircrews have the most current information pertaining to the location of SOF, friendly ground forces, and no-strike target lists.

ELEMENTS OF EFFECTIVE AI OPERATIONS

In addition to the elements of effective counterland operations previously discussed, there are particular considerations that are especially applicable to AI operations. These include the elements normally required to successfully prosecute AI operations (integration with surface maneuver and effective C2 systems) and those desired effects of typical interdiction operations (channeled enemy movements, high rates of consumption, logistics constriction, and urgent movement). To what degree each element contributes to the operation varies with the nature of the conflict, geographic location, weather, and characteristics of the enemy.

Integration with Surface Maneuver

An important factor in successful AI operations is integrating air maneuver with surface maneuver. Planning and conducting AI and surface operations within a coherent framework enhances their synergistic effect in those operations involving air, space, and surface forces. Proper integration can create a dilemma for the enemy commander as he reacts to the resulting combined and complementary effects of air and surface combat power. Two complementary maneuver schemes serve as an example. The first involves airpower fixing enemy surface forces, thus allowing ground forces to engage. Airpower can hold enemy ground forces in place leaving friendly land forces free to maneuver. If the enemy counters surface maneuver with movement, losses from air attack (due to reduced concealment, greater detectability, and increased predictability) may become unacceptable. As a result, measures required to minimize losses from AI leave the enemy more susceptible to defeat by friendly surface forces. The second scheme involves surface forces fixing enemy forces, thus allowing airpower to engage the enemy. An actual or threatened surface advance can force an enemy to respond with counter maneuvers or resupply. By placing sustained pressure on the enemy, surface combat increases target acquisition by flushing the enemy from concealment thereby enabling airpower to destroy enemy forces at a faster rate than can be replaced. Close coordination among all components will help maximize enemy vulnerability to AI.

Mission-type orders allow for the optimum employment of air and space forces by maximizing effects and increasing employment flexibility. For example, using broad guidance, the JFC may direct theater-wide interdiction of all enemy second echelon forces. The CFACC can then conduct a tailored interdiction effort against those forces with specific targeting guidance being developed at the component or even tactical level. In another example, the land component commander might indicate to the CFACC that delay or disruption of a particular enemy ground force is the highest priority for air support. The CFACC can then determine the best way to achieve those desired effects, since he has the best means for determining how to attack the enemy with air and space power. Surface commanders requesting supporting AI should clearly state how it will enable or enhance their operations, listing both the desired effects and effects to be avoided. The latter might include consequences of destroying LOCs critical to the ground scheme of maneuver or the hazards associated with air-delivered cluster munitions and mines. Airmen at the tactical and operational levels, especially those in the field advising the ground component on proper use of air and space power, can facilitate the commander's intent process by ensuring that air support requests clearly state the desired effects.

Sustained and Concentrated Pressure on the Enemy

Two key characteristics of successful counterland operations are sustained and concentrated efforts. AI especially demands sustained, persistent action. Success or failure often comes down to the balance between the enemy's ability to repair the damage versus friendly ability to inflict more damage to the system being interdicted. Sustained pressure can be applied at the source (through strategic attack), at the delivery end (on the battlefield), and through AI against the forces and infrastructure in between. Therefore, persistence is a critical element in ensuring the prolonged effect of both AI and CAS. Eventually, resourceful enemies may potentially circumvent even the most prolonged effects of air attack. Effective employment of ISR assets provides critical information to the CFACC on the results of the opening attacks and on the effect achieved over time by the air and space operation as a whole. Such information will be used in reattack decisions and in deciding when to attack follow-on targets while the enemy attempts to recover from the original attacks. AI is often directed against replaceable systems (vehicles, weapons, POL, communications systems) and repairable systems such as bridges or railroad lines. Therefore, pressure should be sufficient to impede efforts to replace or repair affected targets and cause stress on the entire enemy operation. This requirement applies particularly to operations of long duration, because time normally allows the enemy to restore losses. Attacks on key repair and replacement assets may be advisable if such targets represent the weak link in the enemy's support infrastructure. Concentrating the effects of counterland operations against critical targets is essential due to the generally limited numbers of AI and CAS-capable assets.

A thorough assessment of the enemy's ability to reconstitute or work around air interdiction damage is vital to success.

Accurate, Timely, and Relevant Intelligence

Accurate information about the enemy's support characteristics, force structure, and ability to adapt is imperative to successful AI. Accurate, timely, and relevant intelligence provides information about the enemy's probable course(s) of action, identifies interrelated target systems, allows the CFACC to anticipate enemy actions, and facilitates correct assessment. A prerequisite for planning counterland operations is an understanding of the capabilities and limitations of the enemy and how the enemy is most likely to fight. Accurate intelligence allows commanders to develop achievable objectives, select appropriate targets, apply the appropriate weapon and delivery systems, and keep abreast of the enemy's response. In order to accomplish this, commanders require information systems that facilitate exploitation and dissemination of real-time and near real-time intelligence. Such intelligence is particularly useful in dealing with targets that may have near or immediate effect on surface forces or whose location was not accurately known. Intelligence operations must support the joint counterland effort to enhance unity of effort. To that end, AI targets must be identified and then prioritized in relation to their importance in achieving campaign objectives.

An army can be defeated by one of two main alternative means—not necessarily mutually exclusive: We can strike at the enemy's troops themselves, either by killing them or preventing them from being in the right place at the right time; or we can ruin their fighting efficiency by depriving them of their supplies of food and war material of all kinds on which they depend for existence as a fighting force.

— Wing Commander J. C. Slessor,
***Air Power and Armies,* 1936**

SUMMARY

AI represents a flexible and lethal form of air and space power that can be used in various ways to prosecute the joint battle. However employed, certain principles such as centralized control/decentralized execution must be followed to achieve maximum effectiveness with minimum losses. The objective of AI is to divert, disrupt, delay, or destroy enemy land forces and their supporting capabilities. AI can channel enemy movement, constrain logistics, disrupt communications, or force urgent movement to put the enemy in a favorable position for friendly forces to exploit. To be most effective, AI requires persistence, concentration, joint integration, and accurate intelligence. Whether supporting the ground offensive by attacking ground-nominated targets or decisively halting an enemy advance with theater-wide interdiction, AI provides a powerful tool for defeating the enemy ground force.

CHAPTER THREE

CLOSE AIR SUPPORT

> *The greatest benefit derived from the tactical air force was in the offensive action of the fighter-bomber in blunting the power of the armored thrust and striking specific targets on the front of the ground troops.*
>
> **— General Omar Bradley, USA**

DEFINITION

CAS is air action by fixed- and rotary-wing aircraft against hostile targets which are in close proximity to friendly forces and which require detailed integration of each air mission with the fire and movement of those forces (JP 1-02). Employing ordnance within close proximity of ground troops and the requirement for detailed integration are two characteristics that distinguish CAS from other types of air warfare.

- ✪ **Close proximity.** Close proximity does not represent a specific distance. Instead, it is situational and implies a range within which some form of terminal attack control is required for fratricide prevention. Thus, CAS is not defined by a specific region of the theater/JOA. Instead, it can be conducted at any place and time friendly surface forces are in close proximity to enemy forces. For example, CAS can be employed in support of SOF operating anywhere in the JOA, as long as there are friendly troops within close proximity to the enemy forces being attacked.

- ✪ **Detailed integration.** The requirement for detailed integration because of fires, proximity, or movement is the determining factor for CAS. Detailed integration describes a level of coordination required to achieve desired effects while minimizing the risk of fratricide—from either surface fires or air-delivered weapons. Because of this level of integration, each element must be controlled in real time to prevent fratricide of ground or air forces. Procedures should be flexible enough so that CAS, surface fires, and the ground scheme of maneuver are not overly restricted. The range at which the preponderance of effects against the enemy shifts from surface fires to airpower should define the maximum range requiring detailed integration—this depth is a good point for planners to consider delineating between CAS and AI.

RESPONSIBILITIES

The JFC establishes the guidance and priorities for CAS in the concept of operations (CONOPS), operation or campaign plans, and air apportionment decision, and by making capabilities and forces available to the components.

The CFACC is given the authority necessary to accomplish missions and tasks assigned by the establishing commander. For CAS, these responsibilities normally include recommending air apportionment, allocating forces/capabilities made available from the JFC and components, creating and executing the ATO, and other applicable actions associated with CAS execution. The CFACC maintains close coordination with the other component commanders to ensure CAS requirements are being met in accordance with JFC guidance.

CAS OBJECTIVES

CAS provides firepower in offensive and defensive operations, day or night, to destroy, suppress, neutralize, disrupt, fix, or delay enemy forces in close proximity to friendly ground forces. For CAS to be employed effectively, it should be prioritized against targets that present the greatest threat to the supported friendly surface force. Moreover, CAS assets should arrive in a timely manner. CAS that arrives late may be ineffective due to the fluid nature of ground battle.

Almost any enemy threat in close proximity to friendly forces on the modern battlefield is suitable for CAS targeting. However, indiscriminate CAS application against inappropriate targets decreases mission effectiveness, increases the risk of fratricide, and may dilute availability of CAS aircraft to an unacceptable level. Although there is no single category of targets most suitable for CAS application, mobile targets and their supporting firepower (in general) present the most immediate threat to friendly surface forces and thus are prime candidates for consideration. This is especially true when supporting light forces, such as airborne or amphibious units, since they are not able to bring as much organic heavy firepower into battle as heavier mechanized or armored units. CAS provides the surface commander with highly mobile, responsive, and concentrated firepower. It enhances the element of surprise, is capable of employing munitions with great precision, and is able to attack targets that are inaccessible or invulnerable to available surface fire.

The success of both offensive and defensive CAS operations in contiguous, linear warfare may depend on massing effects at decisive points— not diluting them across the entire battlefield. During large-scale ground operations, there are often more requests for CAS than can be attacked by the available air assets. As a result, CAS should be focused in those critical areas where friendly surface forces lack the organic firepower to handle the situation themselves. The centralized C2 of CAS employment is essential to allow the massing of its effects where needed most. This may often be beyond the troops-in-contact (TIC) range, as CAS missions operating there will have reduced risk of fratricide, and enemy forces destroyed or delayed there are often kept from engaging friendly surface forces. Surface commanders should properly prioritize and focus the firepower of apportioned and allocated CAS at decisive places and times to achieve their objectives. Distributing CAS among many competing requests dilutes the effects of those assets and may result in less, rather than more effective air support to ground forces.

CAS EFFECTS

When it is necessary to provide troops in contact with supporting fires, CAS can devastate enemy forces while spearheading offensive operations or covering retrograde operations. CAS can also be used for the purposes of harassment, suppression, and neutralization. However, because those effects are typically assigned to surface fire support assets, such use may represent a less efficient use of limited CAS missions. On one hand, ground commanders should use their organic firepower when better suited for the task before calling in requests for CAS. On the other hand, a ground commander's organic firepower—particularly longer range systems—may not always be the most appropriate fire support asset. Thus, when planned and integrated well, CAS provides desired effects that can be exploited by the maneuver commander. Ultimately, each of the different CAS applications must be weighed against other, potentially more effective, uses for CAS-capable assets such as AI or even strategic attack. CAS is applicable throughout the range of military operations and typically generates the following benefits:

Facilitate Ground Action

CAS enhances opportunities for ground commanders to seize the initiative through offensive action. CAS can facilitate the offensive by providing the capability to deliver a wide range of weapons, massed or distributed as necessary, and by creating opportunities to break through enemy lines, protecting the flanks of a penetration, or preventing the counter-maneuver of enemy surface forces. Defensive requirements to blunt an enemy offensive may also dictate the need for close support. CAS can protect the maneuver and retrograde movement of surface forces, protect rear area movements, or create avenues of escape. CAS aircraft may also be used to provide escort and suppressive supporting firepower for air mobile and airborne forces, and to conduct surveillance and security for landing forces or patrol and probing operations.

Induce Shock, Disruption, and Disorder

CAS should be massed to apply concentrated firepower where it is most needed by the ground commander. When applied *en masse*, CAS has immediate physical and psychological effects on enemy capabilities. Since available assets are usually limited, CAS is applied against targets of immediate concern to surface forces when those forces cannot produce the desired effect with organic weapons alone, when surface forces are committed without heavy organic weapons support, or when the disposition of targets prevents successful attack by surface firepower. When used against enemy targets that are beyond TIC range, CAS often provides support that is more effective to the ground force due to the decreased risk of fratricide and the reduced interference of CAS with organic surface fires. The task of CAS is to provide selective and discriminating firepower, when and where needed, in support of surface forces.

AIR-GROUND INTEGRATION

For joint air operations providing CAS, integration starts at the operational level during the air apportionment process. Whether conducting offensive or defensive operations, commanders plan for CAS at key points throughout the width and depth of the battlefield where they anticipate close action with the enemy. Using JFC priorities and commensurate with other mission requirements, the CFACC postures air assets to optimize support to requesting units. The operation order (OPORD), ATO, airspace control order (ACO), and special instructions (SPINS) provide the framework for integrating joint air operation's CAS into the commander's CONOPS. This framework is crucial to the effective and safe employment of CAS. In addition, component liaison elements (such as the battlefield coordination detachment [BCD], naval and amphibious liaison element [NALE], special operations liaison element [SOLE], Marine liaison officer [MARLO], etc.) should ensure air-ground integration and synchronization through effective communication and coordination.

CAS missions are integrated with the organic fire of surface units to achieve mutual support, increase the overall destruction of enemy forces, suppress enemy air defenses (SEAD), and ensure air support is delivered when and where required. This detailed integration is accomplished by parallel air and surface force control systems that extend through all levels of command. These systems integrate air maneuver with surface firepower to fulfill fire support requirements as they occur and deconflict air maneuver units from surface fires. Augmentation of surface firepower by CAS can decisively contribute to surface combat success during breakthroughs, counterattacks, defense against enemy assaults, and surprise attacks. Moreover, CAS may also be called upon to enhance SOF teams operating beyond the range of organic surface fires, support SOF teams during emergency situations, or support combat search and rescue (CSAR) situations. CAS is particularly important to offset shortages of surface firepower during the critical landing stages of airborne, air-mobile, and amphibious operations by friendly forces.

Whether conducted during major operations and campaigns or lower-intensity warfare, the need for terminal attack control, the unpredictability of the tactical situation, the risk of fratricide, and the proliferation of lethal ground-based air defenses can make CAS especially challenging. When friendly forces are within close proximity, more restrictive control measures are required to integrate CAS with surface maneuver while avoiding fratricide. The fluidity of the ground situation that exists within this close proximity requires real-time direction from a terminal controller to ensure that targets of highest priority to the ground commander are struck to produce immediate effects. Thus, to ensure that CAS is available, responsive, and used to maximum effect, CAS operations should closely integrate with the surface component commander's scheme of maneuver. The mobility and firepower of CAS can make an immediate and direct contribution to the surface battle when all players work together.

TERMINAL ATTACK CONTROL

A need for flexible, real-time targeting guidance and fratricide avoidance are critical considerations when conducting CAS. To integrate air-ground operations safely and effectively, either a joint terminal attack controller (JTAC) or a FAC(A) provides terminal control for CAS missions. A JTAC is a qualified (certified) Service member who, from a forward position, directs the action of combat aircraft engaged in CAS and other air operations (JP 3-09.3, *Joint Tactics, Techniques, and Procedures for CAS*). A qualified and current JTAC will be recognized across the Department of Defense as capable and authorized to perform terminal attack control. A FAC(A) is a specifically trained and qualified rated officer who controls aircraft engaged in CAS while airborne. A FAC(A) can greatly enhance the effectiveness of CAS by providing an airborne perspective to CAS aircraft while facilitating situational awareness, deconfliction, efficient target area flow, and accurate weapons release.

All air- or ground-based operators, controllers, and observers within the theater air control system (TACS)/Army air-ground system (AAGS) must understand the capabilities and limitations of their various methods to accurately determine the positions of enemy, neutral, and friendly positions. The decision as to what level of accuracy, under what form of delivery, and with what weapons needs to be made at the tactical level and can be largely predetermined and disseminated in products such as SPINS and TTPs.

The three types of terminal control discussed below were developed for use in CAS but are not exclusive to this application. While most often applied in CAS with troops in contact, all three types of control can be applied during other forms of attack where proximity of friendlies and/or a need for some form of terminal attack guidance exists. An example of this would be the use of small teams of special operators scouting for lucrative targets deep in enemy-controlled territory, and providing target description, coordinates, and other information as required.

Types of Terminal Control

Recent technological advances in aircraft capabilities, weapons systems and munitions have provided JTACs additional tools to maximize effects of fires while reducing the risk of fratricide when employing airpower in close proximity to friendly forces. GPS-equipped aircraft and munitions, laser range finders/designators, and digital system capabilities are technologies that can be exploited in the CAS mission area. Regardless of general guidance listed here, *specific procedures for Type 1-3 terminal attack control should always be addressed in theater SPINS or rules of engagement (ROE).*

Types 1, 2, and 3 control are the three types of terminal attack control. Each type is characterized by a specific set of procedures outlined in JP 3-09.3. The ground commander considers the situation and issues guidance to the JTAC based on recommendations from his ALO on staff and associated risks identified in the tactical risk assessment. The intent is to offer the lowest level supported commander the latitude to determine which type of terminal attack control best accomplishes the mission. Risk level is not directly tied to a given type of terminal attack control. The three types of control are not ordnance-specific and the tactical situation will define the risk level (e.g., GPS and digital targeting systems used in Type 2 control may be a better mitigation of risk than using non-guided free-fall munitions under Type 1 control). It is important to understand the most important risk mitigation tool is target verification prior to attack. Therefore, when delivering guided weapons, the point designated by the aircraft sensor, or the coordinates entered into an inertial guided weapon may be more practical factors for risk mitigation as opposed to attack aircraft nose position. Only a JTAC or FAC(A) can provide type 1-3 terminal control. The following discussion provides an operational description of types 1-3 control of CAS and matches CAS procedures established in joint doctrine.

- ✪ **Type 1.** The JTAC must visually acquire the attacking aircraft *and* the target for each attack (JP 3-09.3). "Visually acquire" is literally eyes-on or via optics such as binoculars, without the use of third party devices such as laptops or other digital imagery. Analysis of attacking aircraft geometry is required to reduce the risk of the attack affecting friendly forces. Language barriers when controlling coalition aircraft, lack of confidence in a particular platform, ability to operate in adverse weather, or aircrew capability are all examples where visual means of terminal attack control may be the method of choice.

- ✪ **Type 2.** Type 2 control will be used when the JTAC requires control of individual attacks but assesses that either visual acquisition of the attacking aircraft or target at weapons release is not possible or when attacking aircraft are not in a position to acquire the mark/target prior to weapons release/launch (JP 3-09.3). Examples of *conditions* when type 2 control may be applicable are night, adverse weather, and high altitude or standoff weapons employment. An example of *equipment* when type 2 control is applicable is the use of a Predator or targeting pod sensor aimpoint via remotely operated video enhanced receiver. A JTAC who can see a laser spot on the target, or a real-time feed from a targeting pod, may be better able to deconflict an attack from friendly forces than one relying on visual contact with an attacking aircraft at high altitude. Currently fielded technology has the capability to improve the flow of information between the JTAC and pilot. These tools are an additional means to ensure the destruction of the enemy and prevent fratricide, and in many cases are a more reliable means of aimpoint verification than observing the attacker's nose position.

- ✪ **Type 3.** Type 3 control is used when the JTAC requires the ability to provide clearance for multiple attacks within a single engagement subject to specific attack restrictions. Type 3 control does not require the JTAC to visually acquire the aircraft or the target; however, all targeting data must be coordinated through the supported commander's battle staff (JP 3-09.3). During type 3 control, JTACs provide attacking aircraft targeting restrictions (e.g., time, geographic boundaries, final attack heading, specific target set, etc.) and then grant a "blanket" weapons release clearance to meet the prescribed restrictions. The JTAC will monitor radio transmissions and other available digital information to maintain control of the engagement. The JTAC maintains abort authority. Observers may be used to provide targeting data and the target mark during type 3 Control. Type 3 is a CAS terminal attack control procedure and should not be confused with terminal guidance operations or AI. **Missions attacking targets not in close proximity to friendly forces, and beyond the range requiring detailed integration with surface fires and maneuver, should be conducted using AI procedures vice CAS.**

JTAC/FAC(A)s will provide the type of control as part of the CAS brief. It is not unusual to have two types of control in effect at one time for different flights. For example, a JTAC/FAC(A) may control helicopters working Type 2 control from an attack position outside the JTAC/FAC(A)'s field of view while simultaneously controlling medium or low altitude fixed-wing attacks under Type 1 or 3 control. The JTAC/FAC(A) maintains the flexibility to change the type of terminal attack control at any time within guidelines established by the supported commander. Senior commanders may impose restrictions that will prevent subordinate commanders from using certain types of terminal attack control. However, the intent is for senior commanders to provide guidance that allows the lowest level supported commander to make the decision based on the situation. The JTAC/FAC(A) maintains abort authority in all cases.

Armed Unmanned Aircraft (UA) Considerations

Clearance of fires and CAS final control for armed UA need to be clearly established before combat operations begin. The following guidelines are based on combat operations in Southwest Asia that were applied successfully with the Predator UA. Armed UA procedures should follow the same procedures as other CAS airframes in most cases, but there are situations that require additional consideration. The air support request (ASR) process typically begins when a ground commander requests CAS from the ASOC through the Air Force air request net (AFARN), also referred to as the joint air request net (JARN) (see figure 4.1). The ASR process often works in reverse when an ISR-tasked UA (e.g., Predator) locates hostile forces in an area that requires detailed integration with or is in close proximity to ground forces. In this case, the UA operator usually informs the ground commander (through the ASOC or the direct air support center [DASC]) that a recently discovered target may require CAS as opposed to the ground commander making the request. There are two basic cases that an armed UA could require clearance of fires and final control. These cases all assume that targets identified by a UA meet ROE requirements.

◎ **Case 1.** UA on an ASR tasking in communication with a JTAC who is in communication with the ground force commander.

In this case, follow standard CAS procedures. The local ground commander clears and gives approval for fires in the target area, and the JTAC provides final control.

✪ **Case 2.** UA on an ISR tasking that is not in communication with ground forces.

In this case, the UA operator should receive approval to terminate the ISR tasking temporarily. CAOC UAS responsibilities should transition from the senior intelligence duty officer to the senior offensive duty officer. Overall C2 should transition from the CAOC to the ASOC or DASC. The UA operator should contact the ASOC or DASC to ensure the appropriate ground commander is contacted through appropriate command channels. If the local ground commander has an available JTAC, the ASOC or DASC should provide a C2 and datalink frequency for the UA operator to facilitate clearance of fires.

Terminal attack control and clearance of fires is important to the effective employment of armed UA during CAS. There is an increased chance of fratricide, mid-air collision, and confusion if procedures are not clearly defined. These risks are further increased with the increase of armed UA. It must be made clear that the procedures listed above are specific to past operations in Southwest Asia. Because every conflict is different, these procedures may not apply exactly to another combat situation. The bottom line: *commanders should ensure the SPINS include clear and precise procedures for armed UA.*

Verification

Because there is no requirement for the JTAC to visually acquire the target or attack aircraft in Type 2 or 3 control, JTACs may be required to coordinate CAS attacks using targeting information from an observer or other asset with real time targeting information. The JTAC maintains control of the attacks, making clearance or abort calls based on the information provided by additional observers or targeting sensors. The JTAC must consider the timeliness and accuracy of targeting information when relying on any form of remote targeting.

One of the fundamental requirements of types 1 and 2 CAS control, especially in a TIC situation, is the ability of the JTAC or the FAC(A) to verify the attacking aircraft's aimpoint prior to clearing weapons release. This is typically accomplished either by visual observation of the attacking aircraft, a laser spot, direct data link, or other verification of the shooter's sensor aimpoint when employing PGMs.

While recent technological advances in weaponry and digital/data link systems have provided significant enhancements to the CAS mission, it is imperative that commanders and operators fully understand the capabilities and limitations of the systems brought to the fight. Descriptive dialog between the JTAC and aircraft will often provide the best means of mitigating risk and producing the desired effect on target. *It is essential that all CAS participants use standard procedures and terminology* (see JP 3-09.3 and AFTTP [I] 3-2.6, *Multi-Service Procedures for the Joint Application of Firepower [JFIRE]*).

CAS Execution with Non-JTAC Personnel

Units that have a reasonable expectation to conduct terminal attack control need to have certified JTACs available. In rare circumstances, the ground commander might require CAS when no JTAC is available. This is considered a non-standard procedure and should be treated as an emergency. In these instances, qualified JTACs, FAC(A)s, and/or CAS aircrew should assist these personnel/units to the greatest extent possible in order to bring fires to bear. Due to the complexity of CAS, the ground commander must consider the increased risk of fratricide when using personnel who are not qualified JTACs and accept full responsibility for the results of the attacks. The requester must notify/alert their command element when a JTAC or FAC(A) is unavailable. If the ground commander accepts the risk, he forwards the request to the CAS controlling agency. This information will alert the CAS controlling agency (ASOC/DASC or CAOC) that aircrew will be working with non-JTAC qualified personnel. See Air Force Tactics, Techniques, and Procedures (Inter-Service) (AFTTP [I]) 3-2.6, *JFIRE*, for a detailed discussion.

FRATRICIDE AVOIDANCE

The Air Force defines fratricide as the employment of weapons by friendly forces that results in the unintentional death, injury, or damage to US, allied, or coalition personnel, equipment, or facilities. Air operations in close proximity to friendly forces require particular emphasis on the avoidance of fratricide. CAS requires detailed planning, coordination, and training for effective and safe execution. Though occasionally the result of malfunctioning weapons, fratricide has often been the result of confusion on and over the battlefield. Causes include misidentification of targets, target location errors, target or friendly locations incorrectly transmitted or received, and loss of situational awareness by terminal controllers, CAS aircrews, or air support request agencies. Items such as detailed mission planning, standardized procedures for friendly force tracking and supporting immediate air requests, realistic training/mission rehearsal, use of friendly tagging or tracking devices, and effective staff, FAC/air officer and ALO coordination, and sound clearance of fires procedures can significantly reduce the likelihood of fratricide.

All participants in the CAS employment process are responsible for the effective and safe planning and execution of CAS. Each participant must make every effort possible to identify friendly units and enemy forces correctly prior to targeting, clearing fires, and weapons release. Combat identification (CID) is the process of attaining an accurate characterization of detected objects to the extent that high confidence and timely application of military options and weapon resources can occur. Performed in accordance with ROE, CID characterizations enable engagement decisions and the subsequent use, or prohibition of use, of lethal and nonlethal weaponry to accomplish military objectives (see JP 3-09.3 for further discussion). It is critical for all involved in the CAS process to realize that their actions can either prevent or contribute to unintentional or inadvertent friendly fire incidents.

Risk assessment is a critical factor in preventing fratricide. As the battlefield situation changes, commanders and staffs should make continuous tactical risk assessments. Risk assessments involve the processing of available information to ascertain a level of acceptable risk to friendly forces or noncombatants. Based on the current risk assessment, the supported commander will weigh the benefits and liabilities of authorizing specific weapons types or a particular type of terminal attack control. Considerations during risk assessment should include, but not be limited to, the following: capabilities of units involved, information flow, uncertainty, communications reliability, battle tracking, targeting information, weather, and ordnance effects.

Proximity of friendly troops is also a key factor during risk assessment. JTACs and aircrews must use additional caution when conducting CAS when friendly troops are within one kilometer (km) of enemy targets. The JTAC should regard friendly forces within one km as a "troops in contact" situation and thus advise the supported commander. However, friendly forces outside one km may still be subject to weapons effects. Although a TIC situation does not necessarily dictate a specific type of control, CAS participants must carefully weigh the types of terminal attack control, aircraft delivery parameter restrictions, and the choice of munitions against the risk of fratricide.

Risk-estimate distances allow commanders to estimate the danger to friendly troops from a CAS attack. The distances are defined by the probability of incapacitation (PI) to ground troops. Weapon size and distance of impact to ground troops affect PI. Moreover, different surroundings such as target elevation, terrain, buildings, trees, etc., can significantly reduce or increase PI. When there is a .1% (1/1000) chance of incapacitation, the distance is considered "danger close." The supported commander must accept responsibility for the risk to friendly forces when targets are inside danger close range. Risk acceptance is confirmed when the supported commander passes his initials to the attacking CAS aircraft through the JTAC, signifying that he accepts the risk inherent in danger close deliveries. When ordnance is a factor in the safety of friendly troops, the aircraft's axis of attack should normally be parallel to the friendly force's axis or orientation. This will preclude long and/or short deliveries from being a factor to friendly forces. See JP 3-09.3 and AFTTP(I) 3-2.6 for a detailed discussion of risk-estimate distance.

Fratricide avoidance is crucial to the effective employment of CAS. Commanders, components, and units should conduct joint training and rehearsals on a regular basis that routinely exercise CAS scenarios to develop the skill sets and familiarity required for success.

TYPES OF CAS REQUESTS

There are various methods of requesting CAS, depending on how fluid the situation is and how much premission intelligence on the target is available. Unlike other forms of air attack, with CAS it is very rare to know the precise target prior to takeoff. It is important to note the difference between CAS missions and CAS requests. The conditions driving a CAS *request* may change right up to the time the CAS flight lead checks in with the joint terminal attack controller due to the fluid nature of the battlefield, while such changes may or may not affect the actual execution timing of CAS *missions*. The ground component may have a pre-identified list of CAS targets, but the battlefield situation often delays the decision as to which target's destruction or disruption is the highest priority.

Preplanned Requests for CAS

Preplanned requests for CAS mean the aircraft flying the missions are scheduled for a particular time or time period, which normally coincides with the anticipated time when CAS will be needed most by the ground component. Preplanned requests for CAS will result in one of two types of mission: scheduled or on-call.

- ✪ **Scheduled CAS** (listed as CAS on the ATO) is the preferred method of employment because it puts the CAS assets over the area of the battlefield where they are needed most, at a specific time on target, and where a need for CAS has been established in advance. Scheduled missions will normally have a specific contact point, at a specific time, to expect handoff to a ground- or air-based FAC. Scheduled CAS missions are the most likely to have good intelligence on the expected type of target, resulting in a better munitions-target match. Although joint doctrine states that a specific target must be identified when requesting scheduled CAS, the reality of fluid battlefield environments makes identifying a CAS target days in advance very difficult.

- ✪ **On-call CAS** involves putting the aircraft on ground-based or airborne alert (often listed as GCAS or XCAS in the TIC) during a preplanned time period when the need for CAS is likely, but not guaranteed. This is a less efficient use of CAS resources, as the assets involved may or may not actually employ against the enemy unless a backup target is provided or there is a plan to move excess CAS sorties to AI within the ground commander's AO. Therefore, commanders or planners should consider tasking XCAS flights with a back-up mission in case they do not use their ordnance for CAS.

Push CAS is a form of preplanned XCAS that provides massed on-call CAS when needed. When a significant number of CAS assets are available and the tactical situation dictates, a continuous flow system providing a constant stream of CAS missions to the contact points may be employed. Push CAS represents a proactive method of distributing CAS that differs from a request-driven or "pull" method. While similar in concept to other preplanned CAS missions, push CAS differs because it is planned and often flown before the actual request for CAS is made by the supported ground component. Push CAS missions are scheduled to arrive at a specified contact point at a specified time, normally in a continuous flow, to provide constant CAS assets available to support the ground unit(s) identified as the main weight of effort. The term push refers to the fact that CAS missions are "pushed" forward to the ASOC, DASC, FAC(A), or JTAC before the formal CAS request is made; those assets not needed for CAS should be pushed to preplanned backup targets so the sorties are not wasted. Push CAS works best in an environment where many CAS targets are available, so the assets involved will likely have a lucrative target to attack. Although push CAS significantly cuts response times, the number of sorties required is often high and the advantages gained must be weighed against the other potential uses for these assets (such as interdicting known targets). Therefore, planners should regularly assess how much push CAS to use based on such factors as available assets, existing targets, and the ground scheme of maneuver.

THE ORIGINS OF "PUSH CAS"

The successful DESERT STORM tactic of "push CAS" can trace its origins at least back to World War II. By 1944, the USAAF and RAF in Italy had perfected a method of flowing fighters into the CAS area on a regular, prescheduled basis. This system, known as "Cabrank" for its similarity to a line of taxicabs waiting for passengers, provided a constant flow of fighters overhead the ground controllers, then known as "Rovers." If not needed for close air support, these missions pressed on to a preplanned backup target, typically a bridge
or other interdiction target of known value to the enemy. The Cabrank system was possible because of Allied air superiority and large numbers of counterland assets, and provided the ground force with very responsive air support. Cabrank response time was as little as a few minutes, while traditional CAS missions that were only scheduled in response to specific requests by the ground force might not arrive for several hours. At left, P-47 Thunderbolts en route to a counterland target.

Immediate Requests for CAS

Immediate requests for CAS usually result from unanticipated or unplanned needs on the battlefield, often of an emergency nature, that require diverting or rescheduling aircraft from other missions. Immediate requests may also result from less emergent circumstances, where there simply wasn't sufficient time to plan the mission in time for the ATO cycle. While this demonstrates that not all immediate requests result in hasty mission planning, immediate requests tend to result in missions that are likely to be less well planned or executed due to their nature and will have an increased risk of fratricide. Immediate requests can be filled with ground or airborne alert CAS, if available, or by diverting aircraft from preplanned CAS (or even AI) missions that are of lower priority. The need for immediate CAS can be reduced by apportioning the proper amount of air and space power to support the ground scheme of maneuver, based on the overall theater priorities. The number or duration of troops in contact may be reduced or avoided altogether with the appropriate level of assets apportioned to AI.

When immediate requests result in CAS requirements that exceed the CAS apportionment, the CFACC may be unable to fill lower priority requests due to higher priority missions or request additional CAS apportionment from the JFC. The decision on whether or not to increase CAS apportionment will be based primarily on the gravity of the ground situation and the contribution to theater strategy being made by the available CAS-capable assets committed elsewhere.

There are several factors to consider before diverting counterland aircraft for immediate CAS requests. First, the aircrew must be CAS qualified for all but emergency situations. To ensure target destruction and fratricide avoidance, CAS requires extensive knowledge and familiarity with specialized CAS procedures. Second, the aircrew should have suitable mission materials such as required maps, code words, and communications gear. Finally, CAS aircraft should have appropriate ordnance—fusing and weapons effects are critical factors when attacking targets in close proximity to friendly forces, and especially so in urban environments or where avoiding collateral damage is at a premium.

CONDITIONS FOR EFFECTIVE CAS

CAS is one of the most complex missions performed by the Air Force. The very complexity can limit the overall efficiency of CAS, but it is the only way to get air support against enemy targets in close proximity to friendly positions. Effective CAS requires proper training, equipment, and an understanding of the strengths and limitations of air and space power. In addition to the elements that facilitate effective counterland discussed in Chapter 1 (air superiority, joint complementary operations, appropriate munitions, and favorable environment), the following factors are crucial to the effective conduct of CAS:

Training and Proficiency

CAS training should integrate all maneuver and fire support elements involved in executing CAS. Maintaining proficiency allows aircrews, sister Service personnel, and JTACs to adapt to rapidly changing battlefield conditions.

Aircrew and terminal controller skill is vital to the success of CAS. Commanders should emphasize joint training that routinely exercises CAS tactics, techniques, and procedures to maintain aircrew and controller proficiency. Combat experience has shown that when CAS is not practiced and proficiency is not maintained, a long time is spent at the opening of the next conflict relearning CAS procedure—to the detriment of friendly forces.

Planning and Integration

Effective CAS relies on thorough, coherent planning and detailed integration of air support and ground operations. The ability to mass CAS at a decisive point and to provide the supporting fires needed to achieve the commander's objectives is made possible through detailed integration with ground forces. The preferred use of a CAS asset is to have it pre-planned and pre-briefed. Training and rehearsals provide participants an opportunity to practice operations/procedures, gain familiarity with the terrain, identify airspace restrictions, and discover any shortfalls. Participants should include aircrews, ground forces, liason elements, and C2 agencies such as the ASOC/DASC.

Familiarity with the local battlefield situation is also critical to the success of CAS. When extended periods of CAS are expected, combat effectiveness is increased when the same units remain tasked to provide CAS over the same portions of the battlefield. This allows the pilots and intelligence personnel to become very familiar with the local terrain and enemy operations, as well as develop closer ties with the specific ground units being supported. This liaison should be strengthened through close contact between air and surface units whenever possible, a job that can be greatly facilitated by the Army ground liaison officers (GLOs) attached to flying units as well as ALOs and battlefield Airmen operating alongside surface forces.

Integrated C2 Infrastructure

CAS requires an integrated, flexible C2 structure to identify requirements, request support, prioritize competing requirements, task units, move CAS forces to the target area, provide threat warning updates, enhance CID procedures, etc. Accordingly, C2 requires dependable and interoperable communications among aircrews, air control agencies, JTACs, ground forces, requesting commanders, and fire support agencies. Any airspace control measures and fire support coordinating measures should allow for timely employment of CAS without adversely affecting other fire support assets.

Flexible and responsive C2 permits requests for CAS, coordinated with the appropriate agencies, to be originated at any level of command within the supported surface force or by elements of the TACS, such as ALOs and JTACs. During stability operations, additional restrictions may be imposed (such as increased focus on collateral damage estimates [CDE] or more restrictive ROE)—therefore, expect a possible decrease in flexibility. The interval of time between a unit's request for air support and the delivery of the supporting attack is a critical factor in CAS effectiveness. Prompt response times allow a commander to exploit fleeting battlefield opportunities and to survive in a defensive situation. The CFACC may grant launch and divert authority of scheduled CAS assets to the ASOC to facilitate reduced response time. Diverted airborne aircraft from lower priority missions may also be used. However, a balance is required between the most effective use of resources and their response times. Effective C2 also enhances the ability to integrate CAS with surface operations, coordinate support, and update or warn of threats to CAS assets. The depth at which the ASOC will control operations depends a great deal on the ability to both communicate with forces and maintain situation awareness on targets, threats, and other factors. The authority to redirect aircraft to or from missions beyond the FSCL should remain centralized at the CAOC, while the authority to flow CAS assets to and from shallow AI targets short of the FSCL is often delegated to the ASOC or tactical air control party (TACP). An ASOC is normally tasked to support an Army unit but can also support units from other organizations (e.g., special operations, coalition forces). It may also augment other missions requiring airspace control (e.g., humanitarian efforts). The placement of the ASOC with Army or special operations echelons under conditions of non-traditional support requires a particular focus on joint capabilities to control the airspace, integrate fire support assets, provide high-fidelity ISR, communicate critical weather forecasts and reports, and provide airlift support to ground maneuver forces.

Since CAS operates in close proximity to friendly surface units, reliable communications are mandatory. JTACs normally provide targeting instructions, final attack clearance, and fratricide avoidance instructions to CAS aircraft. FAC(A)s can also provide this capability and will normally be in contact with JTACs to determine targeting, ground scheme of maneuver, coordination measures, and details on the location of friendly forces. Since CAS requires the highest level of integration between air and ground maneuver, specific communications procedures and training are required for air and ground terminal attack controllers and CAS aircrews. This process can be expedited if the ASOC provides an AO update prior to pushing the aircrew to the FAC(A)/JTAC. Standard procedures and terminology are published in JP 3-09.3 and AFTTP (I) 3-2.6, and may be modified by theater and local standards.

CAS requires interoperable communications between air and surface forces. Mismatched equipment slows coordination of fire support, and lack of secure or frequency-agile radios may lead to compromised, garbled, or noncommunicated mission data. Such simple errors as having the air and ground components deploy with different codes/frequencies for their communications equipment can delay the proper execution of CAS. As with the other aspects of CAS, the only way to ensure interoperable communications in war is to conduct fully integrated exercises during peacetime.

Target Marking

CAS effectiveness is greatly improved with timely and accurate target marks. Target marking builds situational awareness, identifies specific targets in an array, reduces the possibility of fratricide, and facilitates terminal attack control. When commanders or planners foresee a shortfall in ability to mark for CAS, they should request that capability during the planning phase. Marking can identify both friendly and enemy positions in addition to being overt or covert.

Target marking can be accomplished through various means, including smoke rockets or rounds, laser designation, and flares. Timely and accurate marking can greatly increase the accuracy of CAS attacks and will also reduce the chances of fratricide. With the use of low light and infrared systems becoming more widespread, the use of marking devices in those spectra can be more effective than visible target marking, depending on how the aircrew actually acquires the target and employs ordnance on it. When marking targets, JTACs must be aware that there is a potential risk of highlighting their position to the enemy.

Streamlined and Flexible Procedures

CAS must be responsive to be effective. Responsive CAS allows air and space power to exploit fleeting battlefield opportunities. Because the modern battlefield can be extremely dynamic, the CAS C2 system must also be flexible enough to rapidly change targets, tactics, or weapons. The requestor is usually in the best position to determine fire support requirements. Techniques for improving responsiveness include:

- ✪ Effective planning and rehearsal between air and ground units.

- ✪ Using forward operating bases (FOBs) or forward operating locations near the area of operations.

- ✪ Placing aircrews in a designated ground or airborne alert status.

- ✪ Delegating launch and divert authority to subordinate units.

- ✪ Positioning JTACs and ALOs to facilitate continuous coordination with ground units, communication with aircraft, and observation of enemy locations.

Flexible and responsive procedures are critical for effective employment of CAS. The tactical employment of CAS is centrally controlled by the ASOC and decentrally executed at the tactical level. Launch and divert authority of scheduled CAS assets at the ASOC or airborne controlling agency provides reduced response time. Aircraft diverted from lower priority missions may also be used, however, a balance is required between rapid response and efficient use of limited assets. Effective C2 also enhances the ability to integrate CAS with surface operations, coordinate support, and update or warn of threats to CAS assets.

Requests for CAS, coordinated with the appropriate agencies, may be originated at any level of command within the supported surface force. Regardless of the intensity of the conflict, the ASOC will operate the AFARN/JARN to receive air support requests from the TACPs supporting the ground commanders. The air request net permits the TACP at each level of command to review the CAS requests as it goes up to the ASOC (see Figure 4.1 in Chapter 4). This stepping-stone approach allows intermediate ground commanders to filter low priority requests (or requesting units) or use other fires (e.g., MLRS; artillery, etc.) to attack the target, ensuring that only the highest priority CAS requests are reviewed at the ASOC. Because CAS sorties are a high-value, limited asset, ground commanders at each level must prioritize where and when to employ CAS to maximize its effectiveness on the battlefield. This prevents the ASOC from being overwhelmed with unnecessary or low priority requests. The ASOC may develop abbreviated message/request formats to speed the flow of information between C2 nodes. If conducting detached, distributed, or autonomous operations, SOF may have to set up unique procedures with the ASOC or CAOC to facilitate requests for air support.

SUMMARY

CAS is an extremely demanding mission conducted in close proximity to ground forces and requires detailed integration with the fires and maneuver of those forces. Using JFC guidance and priorities, the CFACC recommends CAS apportionment. CAS supports friendly surface forces in offensive or defensive operations, anywhere, anytime, and across the range of military operations. CAS requests can be either preplanned or immediate. CAS requires type 1, 2, or 3 control to identify targets, deliver accurate ordnance, and prevent fratricide. CAS requires specialized training, proficiency, integration, C2, target marking, and flexible procedures to increase its responsiveness.

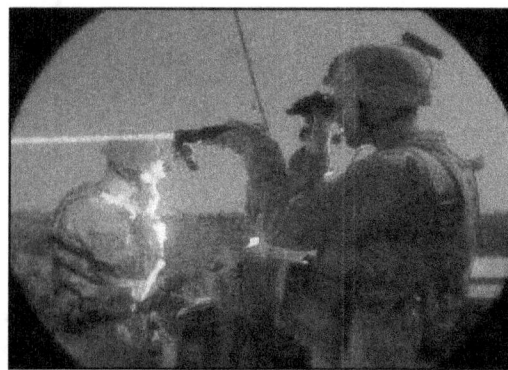 

Successful CAS requires precise teamwork between air and ground elements.

CHAPTER FOUR

COMMAND AND CONTROL OF COUNTERLAND OPERATIONS

> *I will tell you that a commander without the proper C2 assets commands nothing except a desk. You must have the ability to communicate with the forces under your command. You must have the ability to exchange information with them freely, frequently, and on a global basis.*
>
> **— General Ronald R. Fogleman, CSAF, 1994-1997**

Counterland operations using advanced sensors, weapons, and information technology give Airmen an unmatched capability to achieve desired effects against an enemy in today's modern combat environment. Although counterland operations continue to become more lethal, these technological advantages may be ineffectual unless commanders and their staffs understand the complex C2 mechanisms associated with these operations. This chapter discusses the unique command, control, and coordinating elements inherent to counterland operations and describes battlespace geometry and fire support coordinating measures (FSCMs).

COMMAND RELATIONSHIPS

The CFACC's authority, guidance, and responsibilities are assigned by the JFC and include, but are not limited to, recommending apportionment to the JFC as well as planning, coordinating, allocating, and tasking air and space power based on the JFC's apportionment guidance. Since there will rarely be enough counterland-capable assets to meet all demands, a single air commander can best ensure the unity of effort required for optimal use of those assets; designating a CFACC adheres to the principle of unity of command. See AFDD 2, *Operations and Organization*, for a more complete discussion of the CFACC's responsibilities.

The CFACC is normally the supported commander for the JFC's overall AI effort. When designated as the supported commander, the CFACC will conduct theater-wide or JOA-wide AI in direct support of the JFC's overall theater objectives. The JFC sets overall theater priorities, which guide air component objectives and determine the level of support that air and ground maneuver will provide each other. Based on the JFC's guidance, the CFACC will normally establish the specific priorities for theater-wide AI and will apply these priorities to AI targets located both outside and inside any surface AOs. Surface commanders can determine specific AI targets or, more preferably, provide requested effects to the air component that allow more leeway in tactical mission planning and a more efficient use of the apportioned airpower. This way the CFACC can best determine how to support surface commanders who, in turn, will receive more effective air support.

The intent of centrally prioritizing air and space power is to provide the effectiveness against all relevant targets, consistent with the theater commander's strategy. When the number of productive targets exceeds air and space power's ability to attack them, centralized prioritization ensures that lower-priority targets are not hit first, regardless of whether they were nominated by an air or surface component. It is important to remember that all components support the JFC's overall strategy—there should not be great disparities between the various components' priorities for air and space power as long as the overall objective remains in view.

Throughout the entire process, CAS operations remain under the control of the joint air component while supporting the joint land component. The JFC apportions CAS and AI based on his overall strategy and CFACC recommendation. The supported commander distributes CAS sorties to the various functions, areas, and missions to support the JFC's apportionment decision. The CFACC assigns CAS and AI missions to units via the ATO. Ground force commanders request CAS in advance of operations as part of their overall concept of operations and may distribute the CAS to those ground forces expected to require air support the most. While the ground component commander is normally the supported commander for CAS, direct control of CAS missions rests with the Air Force's ASOC, tactical air coordinator (airborne) (TAC[A]), FAC(A), and JTACS.

The surface commander distributes sorties allocated to CAS where his scheme of maneuver most requires them. The air-to-ground portion of the TACS is responsible for providing an air component liaison to the various echelons of ground command and terminal targeting and control who helps ensure aerial maneuver is integrated with the ground scheme of maneuver. The air liaison function should also guide the ground commander in the optimum distribution of CAS among his various units, keeping in mind that air and space power is most effective when concentrated at the decisive points. These decisive points may sometimes be located deep in the battlespace where SOF may be operating.

To create synergy with special operations, the combination of SOF and airpower requires cooperative support relationships. There may be occasions where the joint force special operations component commander (JFSOCC) is the supported commander for CAS and AI within the joint special operations area (JSOA). Normally the joint special operations air component commander (JSOACC) will provide the required C2 elements, such as the joint air control element (JACE), to coordinate and control allocated conventional air power. At the request of the JFSOCC, the CFACC provides elements and C2 nodes to SOF. This may include placing a liaison or C2 element with the JFSOCC, joint special operations task force, or other SOF elements.

There may also be occasions where the JFSOCC is a supporting commander for AI sorties. Whether operating under control of the CFACC or the JFSOCC, SOF and air maneuver elements must be coordinated. Coordination is crucial because air and SOF assets often share common areas and operate in the deep JOA. SOF aviation and land assets are integrated closely in all joint air operations, from planning through execution.

To ensure this, the JFSOCC provides the CFACC a SOLE to coordinate, deconflict, and integrate SOF operations, strategy, and plans with CFACC forces.

Command relationships below the level of the CFACC are exercised using the TACS. Decisions, such as the degree of battle management authority delegated to subordinate command elements, must balance between the commander's intent, communications connectivity, time constraints, and access to information. As with all C2, the CFACC must clearly state what level of decision-making authority is possessed by subordinate TACS elements to avoid confusion.

COMMAND AND CONTROL ARCHITECTURE

Counterland operations require an integrated, flexible, and responsive C2 structure to process air and space power requirements, and a dependable, interoperable, and secure communications architecture to exercise control. The JFC normally exercises operational control (OPCON) through component commanders. The CFACC staff located in the CAOC will task and allocate resources for counterland operations in support of joint operations using host component organic C2 architecture. Reliable, secure communications are required to exchange information among all participants. In joint operations, components provide and operate the C2 systems, which have similar functions at each level of command. The CFACC tasks air capabilities and forces made available for joint tasking through the CAOC and appropriate Service component C2 systems to ensure the proper integration of air and space power with the ground scheme of maneuver. The following discussion briefly describes each Service component's C2 architecture for conducting counterland operations.

Theater Air Control System (TACS)

The TACS is the CFACC's mechanism for tasking and controlling theater air and space power. It consists of airborne and ground elements to conduct tailored C2 of counterland operations. The structure of the TACS should reflect sensor coverage, component liaison elements, and the communications required to provide adequate support. **The TACS provides the CFACC the capability to centrally plan and control joint air operations through the CAOC while facilitating decentralized execution through the subordinate elements of the TACS.**

As an organic Air Force weapon system, the TACS remains under command of the commander, Air Force forces (COMAFFOR). The COMAFFOR's focal point for tasking and exercising OPCON over Air Force forces is the CAOC, which is the senior element of the TACS. In multinational commands, the name and function of certain TACS elements may differ, but multinational air components have similar capabilities.

Army Air-Ground System (AAGS)

Closely related to, and interconnected with, the TACS is the AAGS. The AAGS provides for interface between Army and tactical air support agencies of other Services in the planning, evaluating, processing, and coordinating of air support requirements and operations (JP 1-02). Using organic staff members and communications equipment, the AAGS works in conjunction with the TACS to coordinate and integrate both Army component aviation support and air component support with Army ground maneuver. Army airspace C2 (A2C2) elements are at the senior Army echelon and may extend down through all tactical command levels to the maneuver battalion.

Primary coordination between the TACS and the AAGS starts with the Army's BCD in the CAOC and the air component coordination element (ACCE) liaison at the joint force land component commander's (JFLCC) headquarters. The ASOC is the next level of Air Force-Army integration. While the CAOC provides overall theater control of air and space power, the ASOC provides primary control of airpower in support of the Army. Integration then continues down through the air component liaisons aligned with land combat forces and ultimately provides terminal targeting and control. Terminal attack control of CAS assets is the final step in the TACS for CAS execution. There are both ground and air elements of the TACS to accomplish this mission. When integrated, the TACS and AAGS are collectively known as the TACS-AAGS (Figure 4.1).

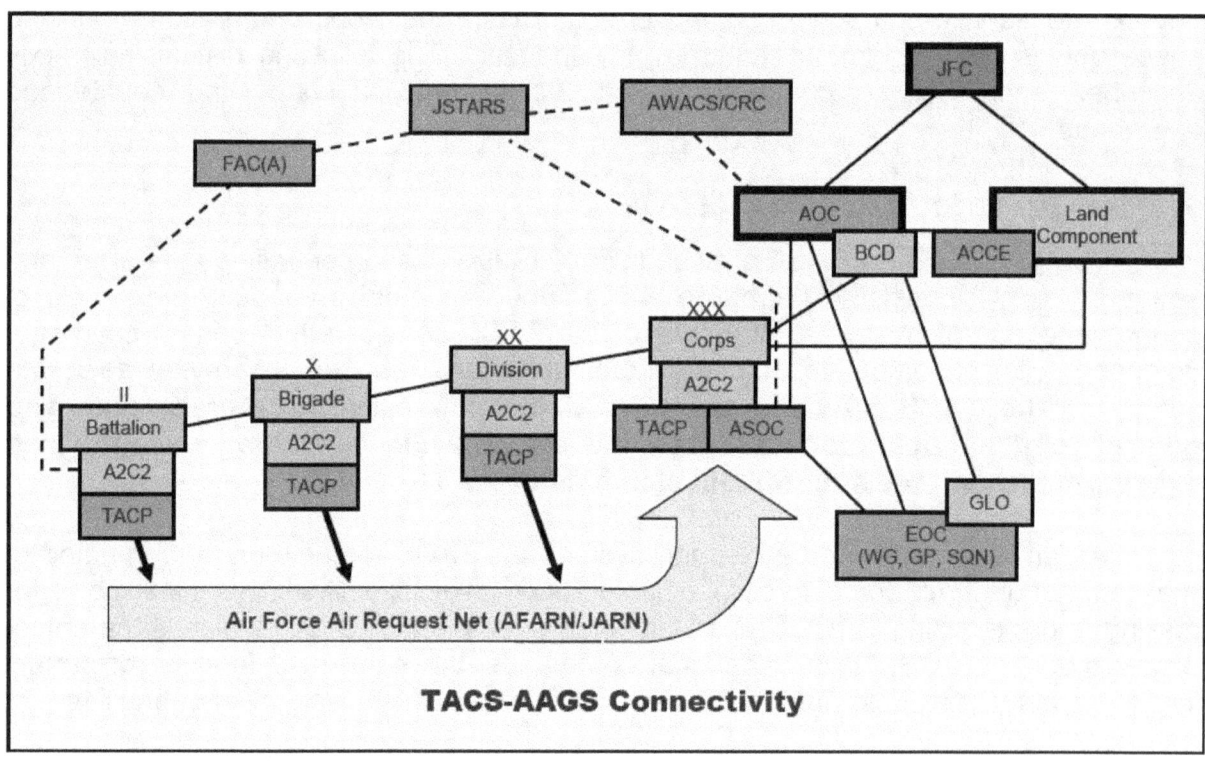

TACS-AAGS Connectivity

Figure 4.1. Key Air Force and Army components of the TACS-AAGS

The Army is transforming its force structure into self-contained modular units that facilitate expeditionary operations. Command echelons will transform to a lighter, lean force. The Army intends to replace its current structure with an organization built around an operational-level command headquarters, a warfighting headquarters, and brigade combat teams (BCTs). As the Army transitions to its modular force, Air Force C2 elements similar to the ACCE, ASOC, and TACPs will reside at appropriate Army echelons. For further details, see Army Field Manual (FM) 3-52 and draft FM 3-91(I) / 3-92(I).

Navy Tactical Air Control System (NTACS)

The NTACS is the principal air control system afloat. The NTACS is comprised of the Navy tactical air control center (TACC), tactical air direction center (TADC), and helicopter direction center. The Navy TACC is the primary air control agency within the area of operations from which all air operations supporting the amphibious task force are controlled.

Marine Air Command and Control System (MACCS)

The MACCS consists of various air C2 agencies designed to provide the Marine air-ground task force (MAGTF) aviation combat element commander with the ability to monitor, supervise, and influence the application of Marine air. Like the Air Force, Marine aviation's philosophy is one of centralized control and decentralized execution. The Marine force's focal point for tasking and exercising operational control over Marine Corps air forces is the tactical air command center (TACC), which performs similar duties for organic Marine aviation that the CAOC performs for joint air component operations. The DASC is roughly equivalent to the Air Force's ASOC, while at lower echelons of command the Marine system uses the same TACP label for air support liaisons as the TACS-AAGS.

During the conduct of an amphibious operation, elements of both Navy and Marine systems are used to different degrees from the beginning of the operation until the C2 of aircraft and missiles is phased ashore. Under the commander, amphibious task force, the Navy TACC, typically onboard the amphibious flagship, will normally be established as the agency responsible for controlling all air operations within the allocated airspace regardless of mission or origin, to include supporting arms. As the amphibious operation proceeds, C2 of aviation operations is phased ashore and command responsibilities for landing force air operations shift from the Navy to the Marines as MACCS agencies are established on the ground. For further discussion of air support to amphibious operations, see JP 3-09.3.

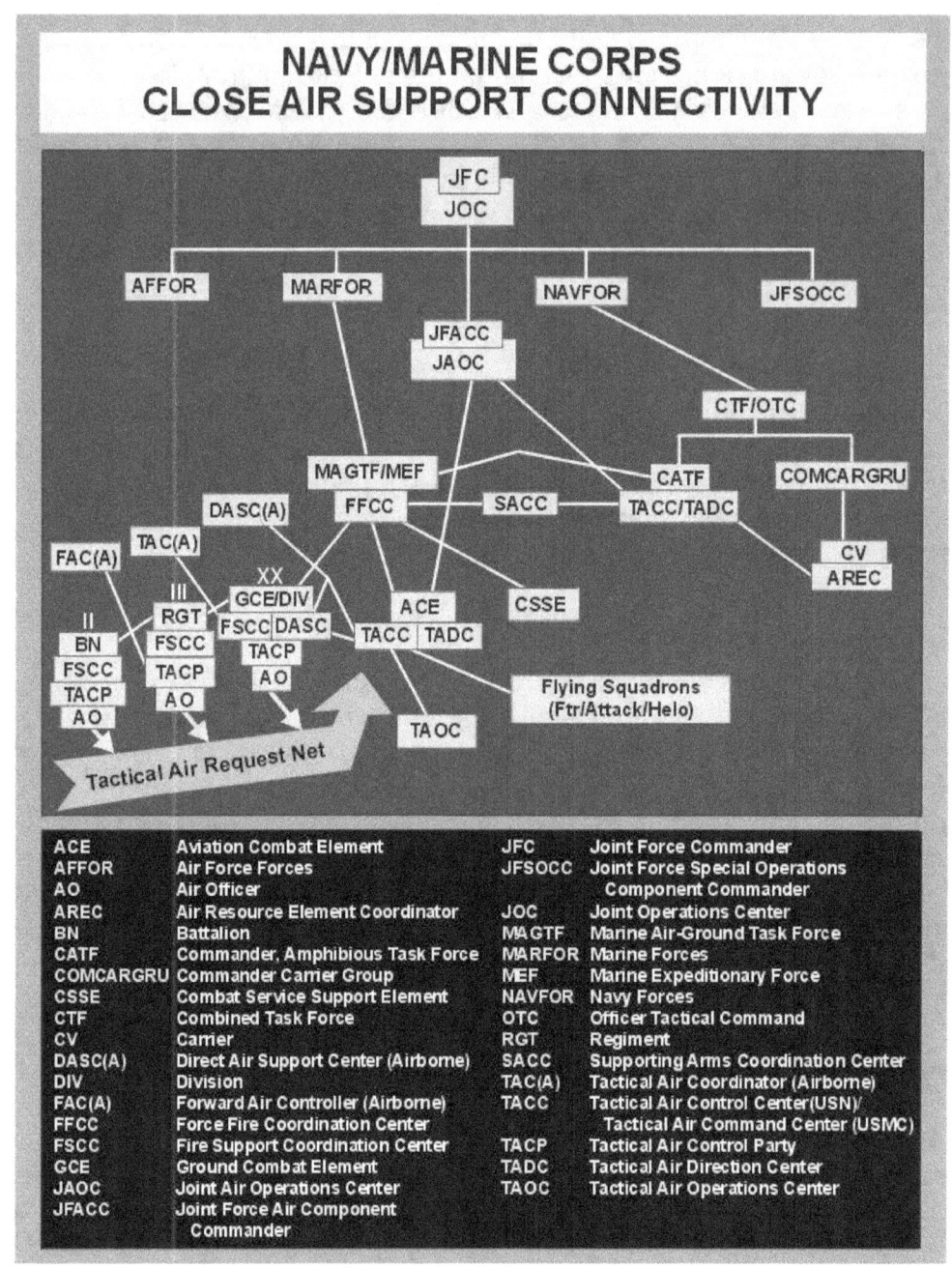

Figure 4.2. Navy/Marine Corps CAS Connectivity (source: JP 3-09.3)

Special Operations

Theater special operations are normally under the control of the JFSOCC. If designated by the JFSOCC, control of SOF airpower is normally exercised by a JSOACC. If a JSOACC has not been designated, then SOF airpower is controlled by its Service component within the joint force special operations command. Principal organizations and personnel that support coordination of CAS for SOF are the SOLE,

JACE, the special operations C2 element, special tactics teams, and JTAC-qualified SOF personnel.

Theater Air Ground System (TAGS)

The digitalization of the modern battlefield has improved the CFACC's ability to command and control air and space power. The speed and non-linear aspects of modern warfare, as well as the precision of today's weapons, dictate close coordination on the battlefield among the JFC's components. The CFACC must ensure all elements of the TACS are in place and the various liaison positions throughout the command chain filled prior to, or as soon as possible after, the start of an operation or campaign. When all elements of the TACS, AAGS, MACCS, and NTACS integrate, the entire system is labeled the TAGS.

COMMAND AND CONTROL ELEMENTS

Air and Space Operations Center (AOC)

The AOC is the operations command center of the JFACC and provides the capability to lead, monitor, and direct the activities of assigned or attached forces. It is the senior C2 element of the TACS and includes personnel and equipment from all the necessary disciplines to ensure the effective conduct of air and space operations (e.g., communications, operations, intelligence, etc.). The AOC weapon system is known as the "Falconer" and will normally be designated the joint air and space operations center (JAOC) or CAOC during joint or combined operations.

The AOC is the senior operational-level element responsible for planning, directing, coordinating, controlling, and assessing air and space operations. Although actual theater AOC organizational structures may vary, the five basic functions performed by all large AOCs include: 1) strategy development; 2) combat planning; 3) combat operations; 4) air mobility; and 5) ISR. Using these functions, the AOC is a centralized hub for developing an air scheme of maneuver, generating a joint air operations plan (JAOP), allocating resources, tasking forces through an ATO, managing airspace through an airspace control order (ACO), and conducting operational assessment. Although the Air Force provides the core manpower capability for the AOC, other Service component commands contributing air and space forces may provide personnel in accordance with the magnitude of their force contribution. The AOC can perform a wide range of functions that can be tailored to a specific mission and scaled to the associated task force presented to the JFC.

Air Support Operations Center (ASOC)

The ASOC is the primary control agency of the TACS for execution of air and space power in direct support of land operations—its primary mission is to control air operations short of the FSCL. Normally collocated with the senior Army fires element, the ASOC coordinates and directs air support for land forces at corps level and below. The ASOC is directly subordinate to the AOC, and is responsible for the coordination and control of air component missions in its assigned area. Located within the supported ground commander's AO, the ASOC's designated area typically extends to the FSCL for actual control of mission execution, and may extend to the corps' forward boundary for planning and advisory purposes. In the latter capacity, the ASOC commander and staff advise the corps commander on CAS employment and target nominations for those AI and SEAD missions that support the ground force and that part of airborne ISR and airlift that directly supports the ground component. Air missions that fly within the ASOC's control area but do not directly support the ground component will normally be coordinated through the ASOC to deconflict with ground force maneuver and fires in addition to receiving target and threat updates.

The ASOC also provides rapid response to requests for air support and is capable of assisting time-sensitive targeting and friendly force location information to CAS, AI, SEAD, air mobility, and ISR missions. The AOC will normally delegate launch or divert authority for alert CAS missions to the ASOC, providing a faster response time when air support is needed. The decision to delegate re-targeting authority to the ASOC for specific AI missions inside the FSCL will depend on actual circumstances, including the timeliness required for getting desired effects on target. Unless specifically delegated, however, targeting authority for all AI missions remains with the AOC.

OPERATION ENDURING FREEDOM TACTICAL AIR CONTROL SYSTEM

During the initial stages of Operation ENDURING FREEDOM, an ASOC was not deployed and established to handle the air war in Afghanistan. This hampered airpower in a number of different ways. Real-time target updates, target prioritization for air assets, and aircraft deconfliction in the target area were often accomplished solely by on-station FAC(A)s. The lack of an ASOC caused counterland assets to waste valuable time and fuel looking for correct/any information on the ground order of battle. Moreover, mission essentials such as frequencies to contact ground forces, preliminary 9-line briefings, or any target information other than a set of friendly coordinates (that may have been 8-24 hours old) were lacking. These shortcomings slowed airpower's responsiveness. If C2 air assets had been made readily available to control counterland operations, they could have filled the void until a suitable TACS was deployed and established, thus improving the efficiency of airpower.

—Various Sources

The ASOC is normally sourced and formed from an Air Force air support operations group (ASOG) and the Commander of the ASOG is normally dual-hatted as the director of the ASOC. In this dual role, the director of the ASOC normally exercises OPCON and administrative control as delegated from the COMAFFOR over Air Force forces assigned or attached to the ASOC. Further, when operating within a joint environment, the director of the ASOC normally exercises tactical control (TACON) of joint forces made available for tasking through an ASOC. The director of the ASOC usually acts as the corps ALO and the CFACC's primary representative to the senior tactical ground commanders. Air Force ASOCs do not deploy independently, and rely on their associated ground forces for much of their logistics support. They may be tailored in size depending on the task and character of the conflict. ASOC members must be strongly versed in Air Force doctrine and capabilities across the spectrum to include counterland, counterair, SEAD, ISR, information operations, and personnel recovery operations.

Three principles should be considered when employing an ASOC. First, an ASOC should not be divided other than to relocate it. The ASOC derives synergy and efficiency from a group of highly trained Airmen working together, in concert. Splitting an ASOC team may degrade its ability to effectively complete its mission. Second, the ASOC needs to be located in a relatively secure location. The firepower an ASOC can bring to the fight dwarfs nearly anything else on the battlefield. If taken out through enemy action, friendly ground forces will lose a significant force multiplier. However, security must be weighed against radio limitations. In order to control airpower, an ASOC needs the ability to communicate with the aircraft. Thus, the third principle is that the ASOC should be located where it can maintain line of sight communications with aircraft to its maximum operating depth. While high frequency and satellite radio enhance the range of the AFARN/JARN, many aircraft communications are restricted by several factors. Radio power, antenna size, etc., are factors that impact communications ranges. Terrain is another consideration. If located in a valley, the ASOC's communication range will be reduced because of line-of-sight restrictions.

An emerging concept is being developed jointly by the Air Force and the ground Services to enhance joint collaborative efforts through complete integration, rather than just deconfliction, of joint assets. One example might be the establishing of a joint air-ground control cell (JAGC2). It would include a functioning Air Force ASOC and appropriate TACP, highest echelon Army fire and effects cell, airspace control, and other Army or special operations C2 elements. The combined actions of these various elements would be the mission of the JAGC2.

Joint Air-Ground Control Cell (JAGC2) Concept

As all Services transform and as a result from lessons learned during combat operations in Afghanistan and Iraq (2001-2005), the imperative to build C2 structures has highlighted both doctrinal and technical air/ground integration issues. The concept would enhance the joint collaborative efforts through complete integration rather than just deconfliction of joint assets. It might include a functioning Air Force ASOC, appropriate Air Force TACP, highest echelon Army FSC, A2C2 and other Army or special operations C2 elements. Envisioned as an integrating cell, the JAGC2 would focus the efforts of the various functional cells on planning, and rapid coordination, deconfliction, and control of all air operations out to the FSCL, integrating the functions currently performed by the ASOC, TACP, and A2C2. The overlying authority would remain the theater airspace control authority (ACA), which is normally delegated to the CFACC by the JFC. Additionally, through fully integrated intelligence, targeting and fires, the JAGC2 would facilitate the rapid employment of all fires while simultaneously expediting the attack of emerging high value TSTs within the ground commander's AO.

The JAGC2 concept is rapidly being developed as an integrated answer to joint issues such as providing C2 for rapidly expanding numbers of unmanned aircraft, and will better enable dynamic targeting of ground targets in the vicinity of friendly ground operations.

—**Various Sources**

Control and Reporting Center (CRC)

The CRC is a deployable, ground based command, control, and communications radar element of the TACS. A CRC is subordinate to the CAOC and provides the CFACC with real-time operational control of forces. The CRC gives the CAOC a current air picture and status of air defense assets through voice communications, direct computer interface, or both. It performs centralized C2 of joint operations by conducting threat warning, battle management, weapons control, combat identification, and strategic communications. It can facilitate decentralized execution of air defense and airspace control functions by detecting and identifying hostile airborne objects or by scrambling and diverting air defense aircraft. In a limited capacity, the CRC can relay CAOC/ASOC information to and from aircraft. The CRC integrates a comprehensive air picture via multiple data links from air-, sea-, and land-based sensors and surveillance and control radars.

Expeditionary Operations Center (EOC)

Similar to a wing operations center (WOC), the EOC is a deployed wing/group commander's C2 element that includes a command post, command section, and other planning and support elements as required. The EOC is subordinate to the CAOC and functions as the operations center for all units assigned or attached to an expeditionary wing/group. The EOC has voice and data communications (direct and secure where required) with assigned and attached units, the CAOC, control and reporting centers, the ASOC, and aircraft within line of sight. The EOC ensures sorties are generated to accomplish CAS and AI missions as directed by the ATO and may recommend weapons load changes based on factors including weapons availability and desired effects. Once tasked with CAS missions, EOCs have the authority to liaise directly with ASOCs and DASCs to ensure aircrews have the most recent information for their intended target area. Using the communications link to the CAOC and ASOC, EOCs provide a critical link for ground alert scrambles, TST, and dynamic targeting information passage. A GLO within the EOC is essential to facilitate an effective interface between air and ground units when conducting dynamic counterland operations.

Airborne C2

Airborne C2 manages airborne assets operating beyond the normal communication coverage of ground TACS elements and can act either as a self-contained airborne command post or as a relay for ground-based command centers such as the ASOC. With properly trained aircrew, airborne C2 performs various CAOC and ASOC functions to expedite C2 while extending the range of radio communications of C2 nodes. Moreover, airborne C2 platforms ensure continuity of operations in the event that elements of the TACS are not yet deployed or have been disabled. Attack aircraft checking in for CAS or AI targets within the land component AO often communicate with airborne C2 as opposed to talking directly with the ASOC, due to radio and line-of-sight limitations.

The airborne battlefield C2 center was an airborne extension of the CAOC/ASOC and functioned as a key link in the C2 network for counterland operations. Although this mission is no longer associated with the EC-130E, elements of the airborne C2 center mission have migrated between other systems such as AWACS, JSTARS, and CRCs. One limitation of this single-platform approach is that aircraft such as AWACS and JSTARS normally have a different primary mission than acting as an extension of the ASOC. For example, their orbit location for proper air-to-air or air-to-ground radar coverage may move them out of contact range with the ASOC. A dedicated UA or near-space communications relay for the ASOC may be a better option when feasible.

COUNTERLAND OPERATIONS AT AL KHAFJI

During the evening of 29 January 1991, the Iraqi Army set elements of three divisions in motion southward out of their static positions in occupied Kuwait. While their ultimate objectives are not known, there is no question that all three advances were aimed at engaging coalition forces, with the largest ground battle developing in the Saudi town of Ra's al Khafji. As news of the initial contacts with Iraqi ground forces flowed into the air control center at Riyadh, additional sorties by E-8 JSTARS surveillance aircraft and fighters armed for air interdiction were ordered.

While JSTARS located, tracked, and provided vectors to the columns of advancing Iraqi vehicles, flights of fighters, bombers, attack aircraft, and attack helicopters from all of the Services closed in for the kill. Close air support was flown in and around Khafji itself in support of engaged coalition ground forces, resulting in heavy losses to the Iraqi 5ᵗʰ Mechanized Division. Further north, the other two lines of Iraqi advance suddenly found themselves very exposed, with their own movement serving only to highlight themselves as targets. Coalition air interdiction missions took full advantage of this, using a variety of night vision devices and precision guided munitions to inflict even greater damage and stop the Iraqi advance. After losing hundreds of vehicles and taking thousands of casualties, the Iraqis abandoned the attack as a costly failure. Airpower assets like the E-8 JSTARS (below left) were key in achieving the results depicted in photograph to the right.

○ **Joint Surveillance Target Attack Radar System.** JSTARS is an airborne joint surveillance, targeting, and battle management C2 system designed to provide near real-time, wide-area surveillance and targeting information on moving and stationary ground targets. It is a key link in the C2 network for counterland operations. JSTARS is a theater-wide C2 platform that conducts ground surveillance to develop an understanding of the enemy situation and supports counterland attack operations. However, the JFC determines the most effective use of JSTARS based on the situation and the concept of operations. JSTARS is also capable of supporting air operations to include AI, CAS, offensive counterair, and other special missions spanning the range of military operations. JSTARS' mission priorities are established by the JFC based on the overall campaign objectives. The system has both airborne and ground-based segments. It is equipped with communications and battle management displays, and can host a CAOC element and/or perform some ASOC functions.

- ✪ **Airborne Warning and Control System (AWACS).** AWACS is an airborne radar control and battle management element of the TACS. It has the ability to provide detection and control of aircraft below and beyond the coverage of ground-based radar, or when ground-based radar elements are not available. In a limited capacity, AWACS can perform the roles of an alternate control and reporting center, alternate CAOC combat operations division, and can relay ASOC information to and from aircraft as well as perform limited additional ASOC functions.

- ✪ **Unmanned aircraft (UA).** Besides their proven ISR, target cueing, and weapons capability, UA can act as a communications link when equipped with appropriate communications gear. This can be very useful in small-scale operations or stability operations when low-density, high-demand (LDHD) aircraft such as AWACS or JSTARS are unavailable. Without LDHD C2 platforms in theater and confronted with line-of-sight radio limitations, commanders should consider dedicating some UA for C2 support to provide the vital link between the ASOC and inbound combat aircraft tasked for CAS.

LIAISON ELEMENTS

Effective liaison coordination is crucial to successful counterland operations. Liaisons within the CAOC include the NALE, the MARLO, and the SOLE. In addition to coordinating targeting processes, these liaison functions are vital for coordinating kill box deconfliction. In the rare instance that a non-Air Force CFACC is designated, the COMAFFOR should assign an Air Force liaison element to the CAOC.

Battlefield Coordination Detachment (BCD)

The commander, Army forces' (COMARFOR's) liaison element to the CFACC is the BCD located in the CAOC. The BCD facilitates the direct coordination between tactical air and Army units for scheduled CAS planning. The BCD also processes the COMARFOR's AI target nominations and acts throughout planning and execution to ensure proper representation of ground component priorities in the overall process. Moreover, the BCD should inform the Army force commander of which nominated targets that were or were not included on the target list for incorporation into the ATO, and the approval status of preplanned CAS requests. This feedback loop is critical, as land commanders must know which requested targets did/did not meet the JFC's priority requirements for air attack. During the execution process, the BCD provides current land picture information to the CAOC on both friendly and enemy ground forces.

Air Component Coordination Element (ACCE)

When required, the CFACC may establish and deploy an ACCE to other functional component commanders' headquarters (especially the land component) and/or to the JFC's headquarters to better integrate air and space operations across the overall joint force. The ACCE director is the CFACC's personal liaison and primary representative to the other commanders in the operation. The ACCE director derives all of his or her authority from the CFACC. The ACCE team facilitates interaction and communication between the respective staffs, but should not be used for formal request and coordination processes such as those employed by the BCD.

The ACCE team reaches back to their respective counterparts in the CAOC to provide the other headquarters commander information on the best way to employ air and space power. This is a two-way relationship in that the ACCE not only provides information and flow to the CFACC but must also help ensure CFACC information is flowing to and understood by the JFC, JFLCC, JFMCC, and JFSOCC.

The ACCE is task organized to best serve the CFACC's range of operations. Generally, the ACCE should include functional areas such as operations, plans, and intelligence and, depending on the operation, may also include a logistics, a mobility, and/or a space functional area. For major operations and campaigns with a 24-hour battle rhythm, the ACCE should have sufficient personnel to work each of the duty shifts. For smaller operations, the ACCE may have as few as one person performing both the operations and plans functions and one person performing the intelligence function.

While a relatively new concept, the ACCE has proven valuable in large-scale operations, counterinsurgency, and humanitarian operations. For more guidance on the ACCE, see AFDD 2, *Operations and Organization,* and the *ACCE Handbook.*

Ground Liaison Officer (GLO)

The primary function of the GLO is to provide liaison between land elements and air elements providing air support to the JFLCC. GLOs are usually assigned to air wings and operate out of an EOC when the wing is deployed forward. The GLO reports to the BCD, interprets the land battle for the EOC, assists tactical planning coordination between the flying unit and supported ground unit(s), briefs aircrew, and relays mission results to the BCD.

Air Liaison Officer (ALO)

An ALO is a rated officer, aligned with a land maneuver unit, who functions as the primary advisor to individual land commanders on the capabilities and limitations of air power. Acting as a land commander's expert on air and space operations, ALOs must be involved in the supported land commander's military decision-making process so they can perform detailed air support planning with their own staff. ALOs are assigned to all land maneuver units at the corps, division, and brigade levels. Battalion ALOs (BALOs) are highly experienced enlisted JTACs who normally perform this function at the battalion level.

Tactical Air Control Party (TACP)

The TACP is the principal Air Force liaison element aligned with Army maneuver units from corps through battalion. The primary mission of corps through brigade-level TACPs is to advise their respective land commanders on the capabilities and limitations of air and space power as well as assist the ground commander in planning, requesting, and coordinating CAS. At the battalion level, TACPs are normally organized to request and control aircraft. The TACP is the CFACC's primary representative to the tactical land commander and provides terminal attack control. In the TACS chain of command, TACPs are under ASOC control. While they operate in the field, colocated with the ground units they support, TACP personnel remain under the OPCON of the COMAFFOR.

TERMINAL ATTACK CONTROL

Joint Terminal Attack Controller (JTAC)

The JTAC is the TACP terminal air control expert. The JTAC provides recommendations on the integration of CAS with the ground commander's scheme of maneuver. JTACs are qualified to perform terminal attack control of individual CAS missions. A JTAC should be trained to: 1) know the enemy situation, selected targets, and location of friendly units; 2) know the supported unit's plans, position, and needs; 3) validate targets of opportunity; 4) advise the commander on proper employment of air assets; 5) submit immediate requests for CAS; 6) control CAS with supported commander's approval; and 7) perform battle damage assessment (BDA). Only specially trained and certified individuals are authorized to perform this duty. JTACs must receive clearance from the land maneuver commander whom they are attached to before authorizing aircraft to expend ordnance.

Joint Fires Observer (JFO)

A JFO is a trained and qualified Service member who can request, adjust, and control surface-to-surface fires, provide targeting information in support of types 2 and 3 CAS terminal attack controls, and perform autonomous terminal guidance operations. Trained JFOs, in conjunction with JTACs, assist maneuver commanders with timely planning, synchronization, and responsive execution of joint fires and effects. *The intent of a JFO is to add joint warfighting capability, not circumvent the need for qualified JTACs.* JFOs expand the target set available to ground commanders by passing accurate targeting information to both the JTAC and aircrew.

Special Tactics Team (STT)

Air Force STTs are composed primarily of special operations combat control and pararescue personnel. Combat control personnel are JTAC-qualified and support SOF ground elements by providing air-ground interface, fire support, target designation, C2 communications, airfield survey, and terminal control operations.

Forward Air Controller (Airborne) (FAC[A])

The FAC(A) is an airborne extension of the TACP. Only specially trained and certified aircrews are authorized to perform this duty, as it requires detailed knowledge of friendly and target locations, artillery, available aircraft weapons and fuel states, the ability to conduct all three types of terminal attack control, and the flexibility to prioritize and adjust in a dynamic environment. FAC(A)s must receive land maneuver commander clearance, normally through the TACP, before expending or authorizing other aircraft to expend ordnance. The FAC(A) may provide terminal control, relay CAS briefings, provide immediate target and threat reconnaissance, and mark targets for attacking aircraft. Threats and weather permitting, the FAC(A) can see well beyond the visual range of ground-based JTACs. The FAC(A) can perform tactical battle management by cycling aircraft through the target area, while prioritizing targets in coordination with the JTAC. In this role, the FAC(A) is operating as a TAC(A). The FAC(A) may provide positive identification (PID), CDE, and immediate BDA.

Tactical Air Coordinator (Airborne) (TAC[A])

A TAC(A) is "an officer who coordinates, from an aircraft, the actions of other aircraft engaged in air support of ground or sea forces" (JP 1-02). Normally performed by an officer on a JSTARS or as a FAC(A), the TAC(A) provides a communication relay between the TACP and attack aircraft as well as other agencies of the TACS. It also expedites CAS aircraft-to-FAC hand-off during heavy CAS operations. Air Force two-ship FAC(A) flights, especially in higher threat environments, may divide responsibilities so that one aircraft fills the normal FAC(A) role while the second becomes a TAC(A).

Special Operations Liaison Element

The SOLE is a team provided by the JFSOCC to integrate and synchronize special operations air, surface, and subsurface operations with conventional air operations. The SOLE director places SOF ground, maritime, and air liaison personnel in divisions of the CAOC providing a SOF presence that is aware of the activities of SOF units in the field and visibility of SOF operations in the air tasking order and the airspace control order. The SOLE coordinates appropriate fire support coordinating measures, targeting, and airspace to integrate and synchronize fires to avoid duplication and fratricide.

BATTLESPACE GEOMETRY AND COORDINATION

Since counterland is normally conducted in conjunction with friendly land forces, FSCMs must be established to integrate joint fires and avoid fratricide. During major operations and campaigns, FSCMs are established for adjacent lanes of maneuver and are linear in nature. Major operations may also involve rapidly advancing ground maneuver or widely distributed ground operations; either of these approaches will require non-linear FSCMs. Moreover, when conducting stability operations, the linear battlespace also tends to dissolve into pockets of dispersed operations and noncontiguous AOs. Since counterland is applicable across the entire spectrum of war,

CAS and AI require FSCMs that are flexible, simple, effective, and relevant to conflicts characterized by linear and nonlinear operations. Before discussing coordination measures, a brief background on battlespace geometry will provide a better understanding for the types of FSCMs required in linear and nonlinear operations.

Contiguous and Noncontiguous Operations

Operational areas may be contiguous or noncontiguous. When they are contiguous, a boundary separates them. When operational areas are noncontiguous, they do not share a boundary; the concept of operations links the elements of the force. A noncontiguous operational area normally is characterized by a 360-degree boundary. The higher headquarters is responsible for the area between noncontiguous operational areas (JP 3-0, *Joint Operations*).

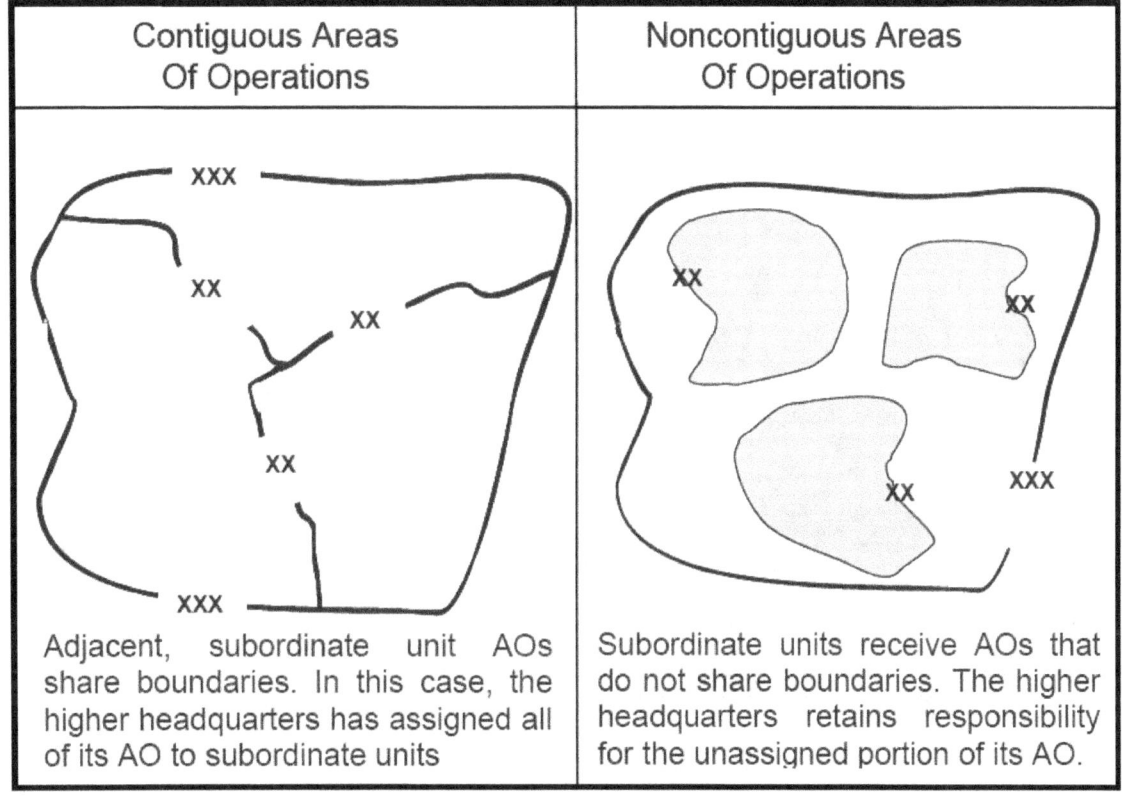

Figure 4.3. Contiguous vs. Noncontiguous Operations (Depicted as a Corps AO)

Linear and Nonlinear Operations

In linear operations, commanders direct and sustain combat power toward enemy forces in concert with adjacent units. Linearity refers primarily to the conduct of operations along lines of operations with identified forward lines of own troops (FLOT). In linear operations, emphasis is placed on maintaining the position of the land force in relation to other friendly forces. This positioning usually results in contiguous operations where surface forces share boundaries. Linear operations are normally conducted against a deeply arrayed, echeloned enemy force or when the threat to LOCs reduces friendly force freedom of action. In these circumstances, linear operations allow commanders to concentrate and integrate combat power more easily. World War I, World War II, and Korea offer multiple examples of linear operations while more recent examples include the four-day ground maneuver during Operation DESERT STORM and the drive to Baghdad during Operation IRAQI FREEDOM.

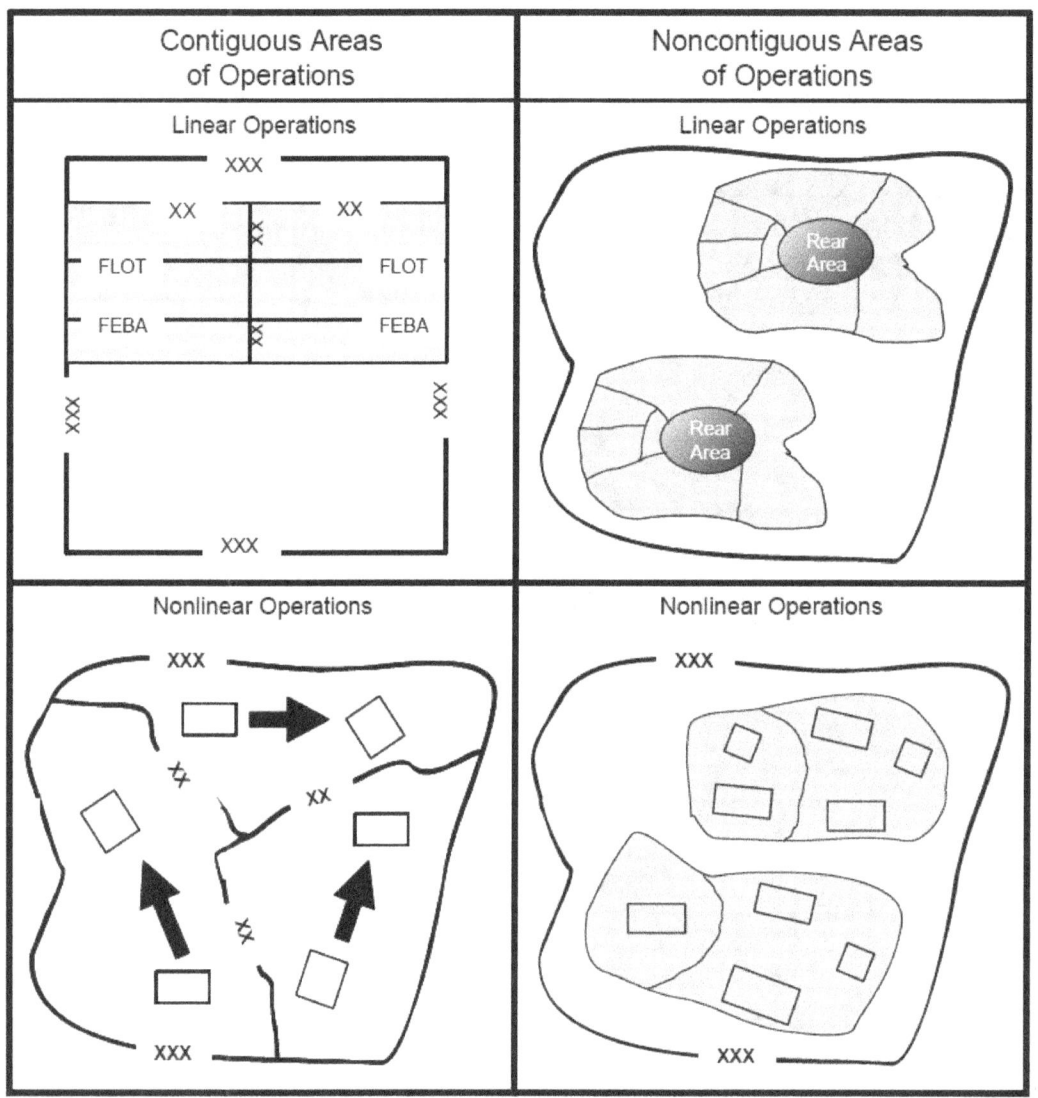

Figure 4.4. Linear vs. Nonlinear Operations (Depicted as a Corps AO)

In nonlinear operations, forces orient on objectives without geographic reference to adjacent forces. Nonlinear operations typically focus on multiple decisive points and are characterized by noncontiguous operations. Nonlinear operations emphasize simultaneous operations along multiple lines of operations from selected bases. Nonlinear operations place a premium on intelligence, aerial mobility, and sustainment.

Often integrated with ground maneuver, swift aerial attack delivering concentrated, precise fire against several decisive points can induce paralysis and shock among enemy troops and commanders. Operations JUST CAUSE and ENDURING FREEDOM are examples of nonlinear operations. The joint forces orient more on their assigned objectives (for example, destroying an enemy force or seizing and controlling critical terrain or population centers) and less on their geographic relationship to other friendly forces. To protect themselves and achieve objectives, ground forces rely heavily on air and space power to provide battlespace awareness, mobility advantages, and freedom of action.

Depending on the situation, the JFC may conduct linear or nonlinear offensive and defensive operations in contiguous and noncontiguous areas. Linear contiguous warfare typically characterizes major operations and campaigns while stability operations are usually nonlinear and noncontiguous.

LINEAR COORDINATION MEASURES

Various boundaries and coordination measures are used for airspace control and fire support coordination when planning and executing counterland operations. The measures help to integrate air and ground maneuver, ensure deconfliction, avoid fratricide, and identify which parts of the battlespace require specialized control procedures. The JFC may define lateral, rear, and forward boundaries to define AOs for the various surface components. The following discussion centers on linear boundaries and coordination measures that play a significant role in counterland operations.

Forward Boundary (FB)

The forward boundary defines a component's outer AO and is the farthest limit of an organization's responsibility. The organization is responsible for deep operations to that limit. Within the JOA, the next higher headquarters is responsible for coordinating deep operations beyond the FB. In offensive operations, the forward boundary may move from phase line to phase line, depending on the battlefield situation.

Forward Line of Own Troops (FLOT)

The FLOT is a line that indicates the most forward positions of friendly forces during linear operations at a specific time. The forward line of own troops normally identifies the forward location of covering and screening forces. The zone between the FLOT and the FSCL is typically the area over which friendly ground forces intend to maneuver in the near future and may also be the area within which ground force organic fires are employed. This zone is the area where air operations are normally executed through the ASOC.

Fire Support Coordination Measures (FSCM)

FSCMs are necessary to facilitate the rapid engagement of targets and simultaneously provide safeguards for friendly forces. FSCMs are divided into two categories: permissive and restrictive. Permissive FSCMs facilitate attacks and include coordinated fire lines (CFL), free fire areas (FFA), and FSCL. Restrictive measures safeguard friendly forces and include no-fire areas (NFA), restrictive fire areas (RFA), restrictive fire lines (RFL), and airspace coordination areas. When supporting the land component commander, airpower must operate within the confines of all JFLCC FSCMs. In order to reduce the risk of fratricide and still take advantage of airpower's inherent flexibility and versatility, FSCMs must be clearly defined, easily controlled, and not overly restrictive. For detailed information on FSCMs, see JP 3-09.3.

Historically, linear operations have used linear FSCMs such as the FSCL. However, as operations move towards being non-linear, dispersed component AOs necessitate the need for nonlinear FSCMs such as kill boxes. Advancements in data link technology and digital information have increased the potential for combat forces to effectively coordinate and conduct nonlinear operations. Non-linear operations require Airmen to continually evaluate the capabilities of the controlling ASOC to ensure adequate resources (manning, radios, frequencies, computer support, etc.) are available to meet the C2 needs of aircraft operating in ever-increasing dispersed JFLCC AOs in the JOA. During kill box operations, the CAOC maintains C2 of aircraft outside the JFLCC's AO while the ASOC typically maintains responsibility for aircraft inside the JFLCC's AO. The following section describes the most significant and controversial FSCM that pertains to counterland operations—the FSCL.

Fire Support Coordination Line (FSCL)

The FSCL is a permissive FSCM established and adjusted by appropriate land or amphibious force commanders within their boundaries in consultation with superior, subordinate, supporting, and affected commanders. FSCLs facilitate the expeditious attack of surface targets of opportunity beyond the coordinating measure. The FSCL does not divide an area of operations by defining a boundary between close and deep operations or a zone for CAS. The FSCL applies to all fires of air, land, and sea-based weapons systems using any type of ammunition. Forces attacking targets beyond a FSCL must inform all affected commanders in sufficient time to allow necessary reaction to avoid fratricide. Supporting elements attacking targets beyond the FSCL must ensure the attack will not produce adverse attacks on, or to the rear of, the line. Short of an FSCL, the appropriate land or amphibious force commander controls all air-to-ground and surface-to-surface attack operations. The FSCL should follow well-defined terrain features or use a common reference system. Coordination of attacks beyond the FSCL is especially critical to commanders of air, land, and special operations forces. In exceptional circumstances, the inability to conduct this coordination will not preclude the attack of targets beyond the FSCL. However, failure to do so may increase the risk of fratricide and could waste limited resources. The purpose, establishing authority, employment, and placement of the FSCL must be understood to effectively execute counterland operations within a surface AO.

The purpose of the FSCL is to ensure the coordination of fire not under the surface commander's control but which may affect his current tactical situation. The land component commander typically sets the FSCL after coordinating with all affected component commanders. All attacks short of the FSCL must be coordinated with the establishing component, primarily to ensure proper integration and prevent fratricide.

Because of this, the FSCL is often used as the forward limit of the airspace controlled by the ASOC. This mandates the various ASOCs and other TACS components have the required connectivity to monitor not only air activity out to the FSCL but also be able to monitor friendly and enemy ground positions, surface-to-air threats, and all other key aspects of situational awareness. Likewise, when the ground component attacks targets beyond the FSCL (such as long-range ATACMS shots against high-value targets) it is required to coordinate with the air component to ensure deconfliction and prevent multiple assets attacking the same target.

The optimum placement of the FSCL varies with specific battlefield circumstances, but typically it should be placed where the preponderance of effects on the battlefield shifts from the ground component to the air component. In this way, the FSCL placement maximizes the overall effectiveness of the joint force, and each component will suffer only a small reduction in efficiency. To place the FSCL so deep or shallow that one component is given complete freedom to operate usually results in the other components being so restricted that overall joint effectiveness suffers. The proper location for the FSCL may also shift from one phase of the war to the next, depending on the scale and scope of each component's contribution during that phase. FSCL placement must also take into account the ground scheme of maneuver and should be based on anticipated, not current, ground force positions at the time the FSCL will be active. History has shown that placing the FSCL too deep is detrimental to overall joint force effectiveness and may even provide the enemy a sanctuary from effective air attack.

OPERATION IRAQI FREEDOM FIRE SUPPORT COORDINATION MEASURES

OIF employed traditional FSCMs. Because of the Army's extensive process required for changing linear FSCMs, moving the FSCL proved to be a time consuming process. Therefore, the initial FSCL was placed well beyond the range of land fires in order to accommodate the anticipated rapid movement of land forces into Iraq.

The deep placement of the FSCL hampered the efficiency of airpower. Ground forces, and their associated TACPs, were incapable of detailed integration beyond the range of their organic fires because no one was able to observe adversary targets. Aircrews were still required to comply with coordination procedures short of the FSCL. The time-consuming clearance process hindered the expeditious attack of fleeting targets beyond the range of the organic artillery. As a result, the area between the maximum range of land fires and the established FSCL created a sanctuary for enemy forces.

The FSCL should be near the maximum operating range of organic tube artillery since beyond that point air and space power provides the preponderance of effects.

The preponderance of kinetic effects shifts from landpower to airpower near the maximum range of organic field artillery. Therefore, under all but the most rapid ground maneuvers, the FSCL is normally placed near the maximum range of tube artillery because air and space power provides the most expeditious attack of surface targets beyond that point. To facilitate a rapidly moving battlefield, a common practice is to establish "on-call FSCLs" in advance that can be activated as the ground force moves. In the past, establishing the FSCL along an easily identifiable terrain feature has been critical to success. Modern digitization, along with advanced navigation equipment such as GPS, has reduced the importance of this factor. When possible, however, using obvious terrain features for FSCLs can still prevent errors from happening in the heat and confusion of battle.

Joint Operations Area

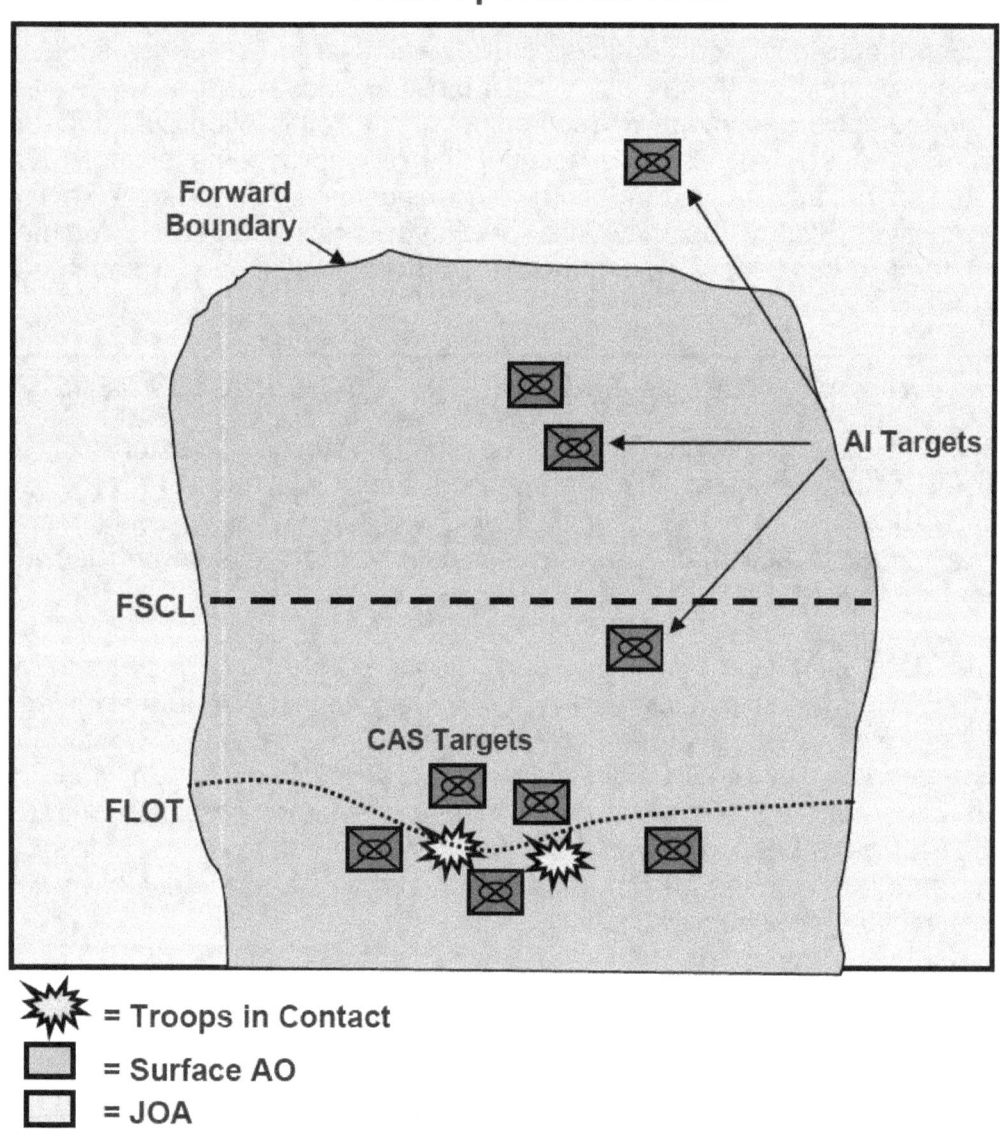

Figure 4.5. Notional JOA with Surface AO and FLOT/CL/FB Relationship

Although normally thought of as a JFLCC responsibility, FSCL placement should be part of the joint targeting coordination board (JTCB) process. This ensures all components are able to integrate and maximize effects in support of JFC objectives. Joint doctrine does not define a depth or range for placing the FSCL in relation to the FLOT or forward edge of the battle area (FEBA). This permits the theater commander to tailor FSCL placement according to specific battle conditions that optimize joint operations. Theater commanders may employ the FSCL to achieve different desired effects.

The FSCL is primarily used to establish C2 procedures for planning and execution purposes—it does not define mission types. Missions flown beyond the FSCL will typically not use the ASOC, as they are beyond the distance where detailed integration is required. However, CAS missions can be flown in the portions of the battlespace beyond the FSCL when friendly troops are operating there and require support. Ground forces such as SOF teams that often operate deep should include the appropriate TACS element for CAS control and have a liaison element at the CAOC. Short of the FSCL, all missions will typically require check-in with the ASOC while en route to the target for an update on potential targets, surface-to-air threats, and friendly troop locations. CAS missions will normally be handed off to a JTAC or FAC(A) for terminal attack control. Even those short-of-the-FSCL missions that usually do not directly support the ground component, such as counterair or strategic attack, will normally contact the ASOC/airborne C2 for situation updates and deconfliction while in the ASOC's airspace.

When the land component attacks targets beyond the FSCL, it is required to coordinate with the CAOC to ensure deconfliction and to prevent multiple assets from attacking the same target. Land forces that often operate deep such as special operations teams should include the appropriate TACS element for terminal attack control and have contact with the SOLE at the CAOC.

Battlefield Coordination Line (BCL)

The Marine Corps has used an additional FSCM for a Marine-controlled AO, called a battlefield coordination line, roughly equivalent to the FSCL for an Army-controlled AO. The BCL is a supplementary FSCM that facilitates the expeditious attack of surface targets of opportunity. Unlike the FSCL, the BCL is used to help delineate CAS and AI procedures, and is highly effective when used in conjunction with kill boxes. Because the BCL is set at the maximum range of organic tube artillery, any sorties flown short of the BCL are typically designated as CAS. This allows counterland airpower to attack surface targets beyond the BCL using minimal coordination procedures with ground forces.

> *The Marines put in place a supplementary battlefield coordination line to speed "expeditious attack of surface targets of opportunity" between the BCL and the more distant FSCL as Marine doctrine defined it. A typical BCL extended 18.6 [kilometers] out from the FLOT—roughly the range of [155] mm artillery. Air strikes short of this line were typically Type I, II, or III CAS calling for varying degrees of control. Beyond the battlefield coordination line, the "kill boxes" could be opened more easily, and the DASC was able to put its brisk procedures into play.... All levels monitored the air requests and intervened only to stop them. The DASC was co-located with [the fire support coordination center], who updated the ground picture as the DASC personnel worked the air picture.... The Marines used procedural control with aircraft checking in at control points to give route headings which the DASC controller cross-referenced.... Aircrews quickly caught on to the fact that the DASC could give them targets fast.... Soon the flow of coalition strike sorties, planned and unplanned, far exceeded anything the Marine air planners thought the CAOC would give them.*
>
> **—Dr. Rebecca Grant,**
> **"Marine Air in the Mainstream,"** *Air Force Magazine,* **June 2004.**

NONLINEAR COORDINATION MEASURES

In conflicts characterized by nonlinear operations, ground forces occupy pockets that may have large distances of open terrain between them (often occupied by the enemy). Under such circumstances, the classic linear concepts such as the FSCL may need adjustment. One option is to create an alternate FSCM based on a common reference system (such as a standardized box, circle, or other easily employed shape) to accomplish the same task that the FSCL performs for the linear battlespace. Although it is highly effective in nonlinear war, the common reference system is also very useful in linear operations. The following discussion centers on using a common reference system and kill boxes.

Area Reference System (ARS)

An ARS is primarily an operational-level administrative measure used to coordinate geographical areas rapidly for battlespace deconfliction and synchronization. An ARS should simplify communications and procedures between the components.

Commanders may use any ARS they deem appropriate, but if an ARS is developed without a lead organization or unified effort, separate grid systems may be developed or used that are not only incompatible but may negatively impact counterland operations. Global Area Reference System (GARS) is *the* ARS developed and approved by the director of the National Geospatial-Intelligence Agency, military Services, Chairman of the Joint Chiefs of Staff (CJCS), and the Secretary of Defense as of December 2005. It is now the standardized battlespace area reference system which impacts not only Service doctrine, joint doctrine, and multi-Service tactics, techniques, and procedures (MTTP), but also the entire spectrum of battlespace deconfliction.

The GARS uses a grid system with a simple, universal identifier recognizable by each component and their associated C2 and attack assets. Three numbers followed by two letters describe a unique 30-minute by 30-minute area. A graphical depiction of the proposed reference system is in Figure 4.6. The point of origin for the system is 90 degrees south and 180 degrees east/west. The areas described by GARS are coincident with even numbered WGS-84 degree and minute lines. Latitude and longitude coordinate references easily define cells since they are common and exist on most military operational graphs and charts. They should also allow for easy interpretation using digital displays common in the tactical weapon systems of all components. GARS is highly useful in facilitating rapid attacks on TSTs and for expediting deconfliction of friendly force locations although it is not designed to support precise targeting. Rather than transmitting a series of latitudes and longitudes, an area can be defined by a brief yet succinct number/letter character string.

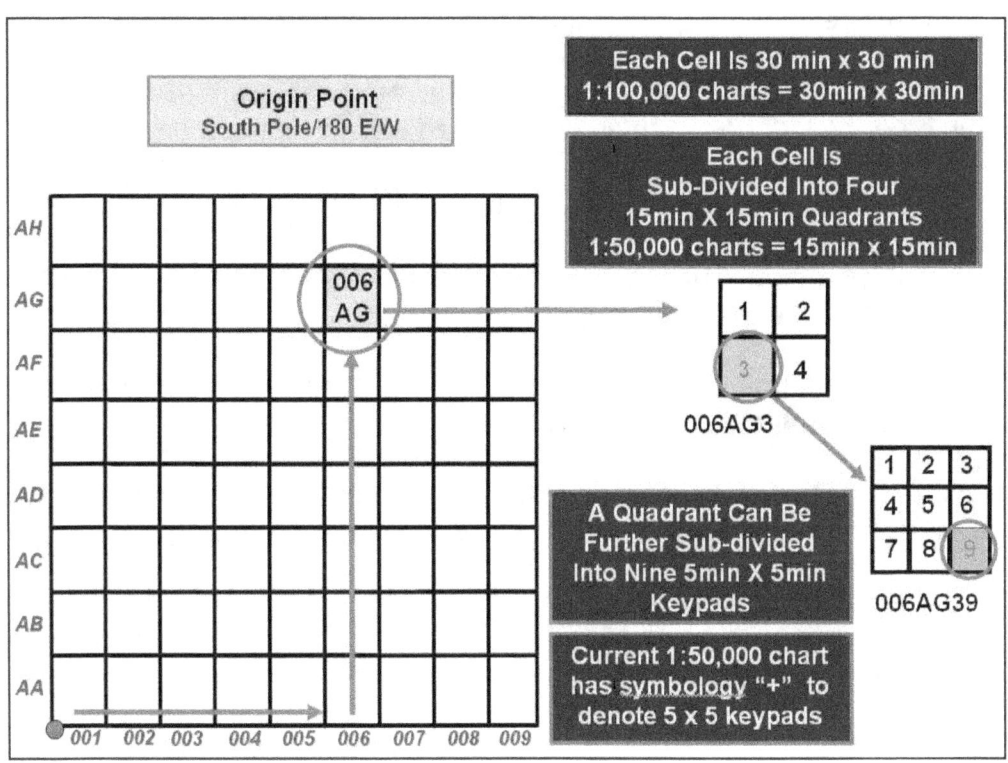

Figure 4.6. GARS Layout and Naming Convention

GARS is also useful because it enables establishment of appropriate control and coordination measures that can be mutually coordinated, deconflicted, and synchronized via a simple, common, mutually understood, and agreed upon reference system. A detailed discussion of GARS is located in JP 2-03, *Geospatial Intelligence Support to Joint Operations.* Additional discussion of reference system attributes in general can be found in JP 3-60, *Joint Doctrine for Targeting*, Appendix D, "Common Reference Systems: Area and Point".

Kill Box Operations

A kill box is a three-dimensional area reference that enables timely, effective coordination and control and facilitates rapid attacks (JP 1-02). It combines traditional aspects of both an airspace control measure (ACM) and FSCM, used to facilitate the expeditious air-to-surface attack of targets, which could also be augmented by or integrated with surface-to-surface indirect fires. When established, the primary purpose is to allow air assets to conduct interdiction against surface targets without further coordination with the establishing commander and without terminal attack control. A kill box will not be established specifically for CAS missions. When used to integrate air-to-surface and surface-to-surface fires, the kill box will have appropriate restrictions. Restrictive FSCMs and ACMs will always have priority when established in a kill box. For an in-depth discussion, see AFTTP (I) 3-2.59, *Kill Box*.

A kill box is established and adjusted by the appropriate supported commander and is an extension of an existing support relationship established by the JFC. Kill box boundaries normally are defined using an area reference system (e.g., GARS), but could follow other boundaries such as well-defined terrain features or may be located by grid or by a radius from a center point. Changes to a kill box require notification of all affected forces within the JOA and must allow sufficient time for these forces and/or components to incorporate the kill box change. When building a kill box construct, the entire JOA can be mapped using an ARS (such as grids and keypads used in the GARS) before the start of an operation or campaign.

Tactical fire support control procedures within a theater of operations may use colors and specific terminology to describe the status of kill boxes within a JOA.

- ✪ **Blue Kill Box.** A blue kill box permits air-to-surface fires effects in the kill box without further coordination with the establishing headquarters.

- ✪ **Purple Kill Box.** A purple kill box permits the integration of surface-to-surface fires with air-to-surface fires into the purple kill box without further coordination.

- ✪ **Established.** A kill box that is in effect, either via the joint targeting cycle or execution period. Information about the time it becomes effective, the duration, or other attributes will be published and disseminated in the ACO.

- ✪ **Open.** Term used to describe a portion or portions of a kill box that are open to fires without further coordination or deconfliction. An established kill box is inherently open, until closed or cancelled. (AFTTP [I] 3-2.59)

- ✪ **Active.** An established kill box that has aircraft flying in the space defined by the box or effects of air or other joint fires within the boundaries of the kill box.

✪ **Cold.** An established kill box that is not active. All portions of the kill box are open to fires unless identified as closed.

✪ **Closed.** Term used to describe a portion or portions of an established kill box in which fires or effects of fires are not allowed without further coordination.

✪ **Cancelled.** The kill box is no longer in effect.

Although use of kill boxes is not mandatory, the kill box system reduces the coordination required to fulfill support requirements with maximum flexibility. Kill boxes support the commander's objectives and concept of operations, including designated target priority, effects, and timing of fires. C2 updates on kill boxes will be accomplished (e.g., altitude restrictions, frequency use, established control measures within the kill box) via appropriate C2 systems. With appropriate restrictions, surface-to-surface fires may occur simultaneously with air-to-surface strikes. Kill boxes can augment use of traditional FSCMs, such as FSCL, CFL, and BCL. They can help the commander focus the effort of air assets. When traditional FSCMs are not useful or are less applicable, the kill box can be the primary method for identifying areas to focus air assets in. Five factors should be considered when building a kill box system.

✪ A kill box is an ACM/FSCM, and is not a reference system. Kill box boundaries are normally defined using an area reference system, which provides the construct (a two-dimensional system), and a kill box is the application. The addition of altitude restrictions makes a kill box a three-dimensional paradigm.

✪ Applicable ROE, collateral damage guidance and restrictions, PID, and the SPINS must still be followed in a kill box.

✪ The decision to use a kill box requires careful consideration by the controlling authority. If used, its size, location, and timing is based on estimates of the situation and concept of operations. The commander must consider disposition of enemy forces, friendly forces, anticipated rates of movement, concept and tempo of the operation, surface-to-surface weapon capabilities, and other factors.

✪ A kill box is an ACM/FSCM that may contain other measures within its boundaries (e.g., NFA, restricted operating zones [ROZ], and airspace coordination areas).

✪ Integration of air-to-surface and surface-to-surface fires requires application of appropriate restrictions: altitude, time separation, or lateral separation. The supported commander will determine which of these is appropriate for the mission and ensure dissemination through the appropriate C2 nodes.

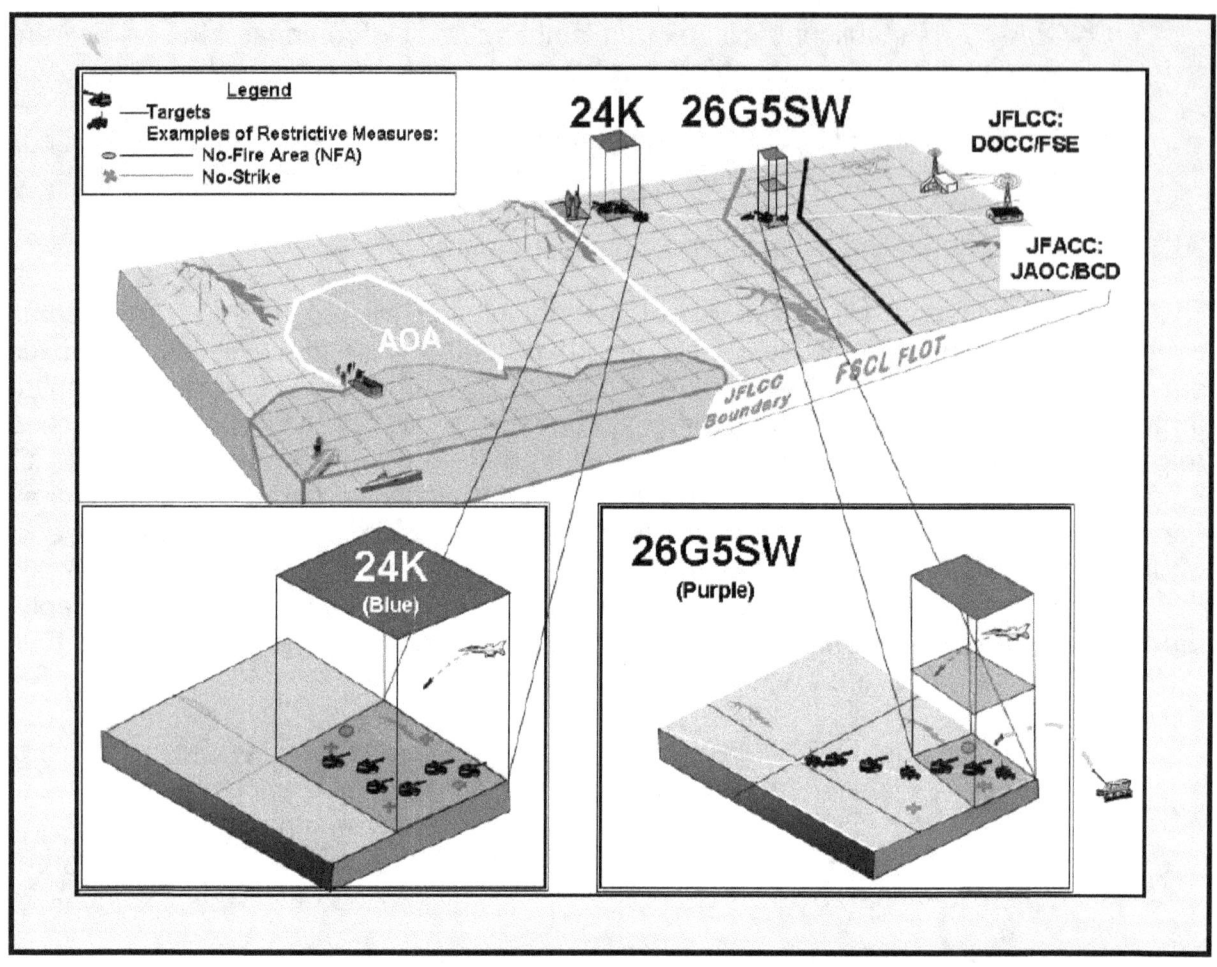

Figure 4.7. Notional Kill Box Construct

The CAOC is the CFACC's C2 element responsible for coordinating fires in CFACC-controlled kill boxes. Other components must coordinate with the CAOC prior to entering or engaging targets in a CFACC kill box. This is normally done through the various liaison elements attached to the CAOC, i.e., the BCD, the NALE, the MARLO, and the SOLE. Through the ATO, the CAOC tasks airpower to enter and engage targets in kill boxes without further coordination with other components

The ASOC is the CFACC's agency for coordinating the use of airpower in JFLCC kill boxes. Through the TACS-AAGS, the ASOC funnels airpower to JFLCC kill boxes. The ASOC has authority to divert airpower between JFLCC kill boxes, but the CAOC retains the authority to divert air assets from CFACC to JFLCC kill boxes or vice versa.

Traditional FSCM concepts still have a place in kill box operations. In place of "on-call FSCLs," C2 measures must be established to quickly transfer kill boxes from CFACC to JFLCC control to accommodate cases of rapid friendly land force movement. In these cases, the ACCE liaison to the JFLCC, the BCD liaison to the CAOC, the CAOC's communications with the ASOC, and the senior ALO interface with the senior tactical land commander are critical. FLOTs still exist in kill box operations. However, as operations become more non-linear, FLOT definition becomes more difficult.

Between the time an aircrew steps to an aircraft and when the aircrew arrives in the kill box, the FLOT may change dramatically. During non-linear operations (with or without kill boxes), ASOC resource requirements increase. However, procedures for transferring kill boxes from CFACC to JFLCC control and the ACCE's liaison to the JFLCC on AI target nominations take on added importance.

The JFSOCC may task STT to support the CFACC in CFACC kill boxes. These taskings may include finding and fixing targets as well as providing laser designation support (autonomous terminal guidance operations). Although these scenarios do not constitute CAS, they do require some coordination. This necessitates that air assets coordinate with the JFSOCC's C2 structure before entering or attacking targets in the keypads.

Combined Kill Box and Traditional FSCM Operations

A combination of kill box and traditional FSCMs is possible, such as when a single large advance is made from a classic linear battlefield (such as operations during OIF). Here the standard FSCL could be used for the slower moving ground forces, and a localized JFLCC kill box system could be created in front of, or behind, a rapid advance. This allows for more efficient air attack on non-engaged enemy land forces, the greatest freedom of land and aerial maneuver, and enhanced combat effectiveness—especially during non-linear operations.

C2 of air and space power in these situations is conducted through the TACS as previously discussed. The ASOC is responsible for all air operations short of the FSCL as well in JFLCC kill boxes. The CAOC maintains responsibility for airpower operations beyond the FSCL and in CFACC kill boxes.

SUMMARY

Understanding the TACS is crucial to effective counterland operations. Air operations are centrally controlled through the CAOC and decentrally executed by the lower echelon elements of the TACS. FSCMs must be flexible and efficient for the successful employment of counterland operations. The FSCL is an important FSCM in linear combat operations while the kill box system is suited for either linear/non-linear or contiguous/non-contiguous conflicts.

Theater commanders are beginning to employ kill boxes in lieu of or in combination with FSCLs to facilitate expeditious coordination of effects. Digitization of the battlespace aids this effort as it dramatically increases situational awareness and will significantly improve the commanders' ability to rapidly attack threats through proper kill box management. Kill boxes also provide one way to do counterland targeting in near-real time against mobile ground forces that defy long range preplanning. The use of kill boxes improves coordination and control measures throughout the JOA and provides a tool to help manage nonlinear and integrated joint operations.

CHAPTER FIVE

CONDUCTING COUNTERLAND OPERATIONS

> *We are not preparing the battlefield, we are destroying it.*
>
> **—Sign posted in the "Black Hole" planning cell during DESERT STORM**

Air and space power has attributes that allow it to be employed in diverse and multiple combat tasks across the joint operations area. However, there is rarely enough air and space power available to satisfy all demands. Effective counterland operations call for centralized control and decentralized execution. The CFACC optimizes the use of normally scarce air and space assets through centralized control. Centralized control also minimizes undue dissipation and fragmentation of effort and ensures coherence and focus on essential JFC objectives. Because no single commander can personally direct all the detailed actions of a typical complement of assigned and available air and space forces, decentralized execution of air missions is necessary and is accomplished by delegating appropriate authority for detailed mission planning and execution. Decentralized execution ensures effective employment of limited assets, allows tactical adaptation, and accommodates the Services' different employment concepts and procedures.

The intent of this chapter is to give commanders and planners a broad perspective on planning and employment considerations for counterland operations. Detailed discussion of the air and space estimate process and the air tasking cycle is contained in AFDD 2, *Operations and Organization*, and AFDD 2-1.9, *Targeting*, respectively. This chapter will begin with broad planning considerations for course of action development and then discuss elements pertinent to each phase of the air tasking cycle.

BASIC PLANNING CONSIDERATIONS

Supporting Counterland Operations

Both AI and CAS operations require the full spectrum of support, from logistics to force protection to administrative services. Logistics and other combat support are key enablers to counterland operations. Key factors affecting logistics supportability include force beddown and base support planning, deployment and sustainment of munitions and fuel, and maintenance support for critical spares. A robust air mobility capability, especially for intratheater movement, is critical for getting this logistical support to the bases that require it. As an expeditionary force, these key support issues assume even greater importance. This section highlights some of the support aspects that are particularly important to the counterland function.

- ✪ **Munitions Requirements.** As the arsenal of precision-guided munitions that can be employed in counterland continues to grow, maintaining proper stocks at operating locations becomes increasingly important. There will usually be tradeoffs involved in deciding which weapons to employ against specific targets, and availability will often be a factor. Proper knowledge of the munitions available at each air base, carrier battle group, etc., along with their weapons resupply capability, is mandatory. Those munitions with the greatest potential for accuracy, destructiveness, or standoff range are often in the shortest supply. Targeteers and weaponeers should keep in mind factors such as anticipated length of the campaign, munitions needs of the various campaign phases, and tradeoffs of each weapons type when making munitions recommendations.

AIR REFUELING—A CRITICAL ENABLER

Air refueling is a key part of most air component operations and extends the range, payload, and endurance of counterland assets, thereby increasing their effectiveness. In some cases, counterland missions would not be possible at all without air refueling capability. As this DESERT STORM photo of an Air Force KC-135 refueling Marine F/A-18s demonstrates, air refueling is a key factor in all air component operations, whether US Air Force, other Service, or allied nation forces are involved. Air refueling is a key enabler to initial force deployment as well, since most counterland aircraft lack the range to deploy directly to or from the combat theater on their own.

- ✪ **Air Refueling.** Air Force air refueling aircraft have evolved from their traditional role of supporting long range strategic attack to become an essential, integrated part of counterland force packaging. Tanker aircraft are a force multiplier that enhances, or in some cases enables, counterland operations by allowing access to a wider range of targets and payloads. Station times will be increased for airborne alert AI and CAS missions, providing decreased response times and increasing the counterland effect on the enemy. One of the key tasks for ATO production teams is to optimize use of the available tankers; availability of refueling booms and drogues is often the limiting factor that determines how many counterland targets can be attacked in a given cycle.

While technically a "support" asset, air refueling has become such an integrated part of counterland force packaging that it would be difficult to imagine operating without the enhanced capabilities it provides. For example, enemy antiship defenses may force an aircraft carrier to stand off from the counterland area, requiring Air Force refueling support to get carrier aviation to the fight. When air superiority is in dispute, and enemy aircraft and missiles threaten air bases close to the ground fighting, air refueling may be the only way to get counterland missions to the fight from protected bases further to the rear.

Target Development

During target development, the planned targeting process should relate specific targets to objectives, desired effects, and accompanying actions. Target development requires thorough examination of the adversary as a system to understand where critical linkages and vulnerabilities lie. Target development involves four distinct functions: 1) target analysis, 2) target validation, 3) target nomination, and 4) collection and exploitation requirements. The product of this phase is the joint integrated prioritized target list (JIPTL). AFDD 2-1.9, *Targeting,* provides information on air planning and the targeting process.

Once potential targets are identified, intelligence provides precise location of individual target elements, status of defenses, and other information necessary for the detailed planning of counterland missions. Warfare is dynamic and demands that friendly forces adapt their methods to cope with enemy responses. The ability to detect, assess, and properly choose targets is a function of several attributes discussed in the following paragraphs.

The suitability of a target set for attack is often decided by a combination of its criticality and vulnerability. For example, fewer conveyances and depots in an enemy transportation system increase the enemy's dependence on that system, therefore, each potential target in that transportation system becomes more critical. Conversely, an enemy possessing a varied, dispersed transportation system is less operationally vulnerable to infrastructure interdiction. Tactical vulnerability refers to the ease of attacking a particular target, based on hardening, defenses, etc., once it has been identified that the attack will produce the desired effects. Tactical vulnerability is important, as the benefit of attacking a target must be balanced against the expected cost. Timing is also key to a particular target's criticality to the enemy. For example, rotary-wing forces typically operate from forward arming and refueling points that are mobile and thus not exceedingly hardened. Catching an enemy helicopter force at such a location could yield high payoffs in terms of both forces and infrastructure destroyed. When marshalling for an attack, or deploying for transport to the forward area, ground combat units may be exceedingly vulnerable for short periods. The enemy may risk this temporary vulnerability in order to get their forces into combat, but proper friendly intelligence can create opportunities for high payoff attacks by allowing planners to focus on the exact time of maximum enemy vulnerability.

Mobile targets will normally require a different approach than fixed targets, whether attacking actual enemy combat forces or their fielded support. Modern sensors such as moving target indicators can often locate and compute accurate bombing solutions for any moving vehicle on a battlefield, and the heat generated by operating engines and equipment often makes mobile units easily located by either onboard sensors or precision-guided munitions. In some theaters, the CAOC employs a dynamic targeting cell to ensure planning both maximizes the effectiveness of counterland attack on mobile targets and integrates the effort with the ground scheme of maneuver. Fixed targets may be harder to identify with onboard sensors and may be more hardened against weapons effects, but their fixed nature makes target location easier and simplifies targeting by weapons such as GPS-aided bombs or missiles.

Environmental factors need consideration during target development. Target area environmental conditions include terrain features, adverse weather, time of day/night, humidity and temperature effects, solar activity, and active or passive defense measures (such as smoke and camouflage). These may act to conceal targets, reduce visibility, and degrade weapon systems and overall counterland capabilities. Lunar illumination and weather conditions can drastically affect the ability of onboard sensors to both locate and identify targets. Terrain features may restrict target acquisition in some bandwidths, thus requiring specialized weapons, sensors, and tactics. The flexibility of different sensors and munitions that allow use of optical, near and far spectrum infrared (IR), radar, and GPS for target acquisition, marking, and weapons guidance gives the counterland planner many options to counter the natural and artificial obstacles to success. However, the flexibility of these same sensors and weapons may be limited depending on environment conditions

During the target development phase, planners should coordinate with other organizations and components to prevent fratricide, collateral damage, or a propaganda advantage for the enemy. Extensive coordination is required with the land component and SOLE to facilitate this. Examples of operations requiring this level of coordination are personnel recovery and information operations, to include public affairs.

The JFSOCC must deconflict special operations through the JFC and with the other component commanders to avoid fratricide. CAOC personnel should work through the BCD within the CAOC and the ASOC to ensure that air and space component targeting is coordinated with and deconflicted from land component operations. Careful crafting and placement of FSCMs can facilitate this.

Urban Considerations

Unless specifically stated otherwise, Air Force doctrine applies to the full range of military operations, as appropriate, from stability, security, transition, and reconstruction operations to major operations and campaigns. Doctrine for joint urban operations, outlined in JP 3-06, describes the triad of terrain, population, and infrastructure that must be considered before and during operations in that environment. Urban warfare is specific to an environment, and should not be substituted with related terms of irregular or asymmetric warfare.

While urban environments vary greatly, challenges to counterland operations can be expected in identification of combatants, collateral damage, preservation of infrastructure, restrictive rules of engagement, line-of-sight issues (to include targeting as well as communications), and freedom of maneuver. C2 of air power does not change in the urban environment, but tactics, techniques, and procedures may be vastly different from those employed on the open battlefield.

Planners must consider that ground operations will be largely decentralized due to communication limitations, and coordination will be time-consuming to prevent fratricide and mitigate collateral damage. Large munitions may be traded for increased loiter time in fuel, as smaller precise weapons with tailored effects are more desirable for employment.

Collateral damage in cities or towns that have not been evacuated will represent a great risk that must be considered and minimized. One real, alleged, or staged collateral damage or fratricide event can have strategic impact, affecting ROE, SPINS, host nation restrictions on operations, etc. Planners should integrate public affairs and psychological operations into counterland operations from strategy development through mission execution. Public information planners must be involved early in the process to mitigate negative events and leverage successes during counterland operations. Next, planners need to account for weather effects caused by the urban environment. Factors include increased pollution and aerosols affecting target detection, warmer temperatures affecting IR signatures, and variable wind speeds affected by building layout. Finally, urban operations, by their very nature, involve significant law of armed conflict considerations. In particular, commanders and aircrew must determine whether the operation is a military necessity and whether the potential harm to noncombatants outweighs the importance of the operation.

CAS will be difficult when supporting house-to-house ground fighting, where the task of locating and identifying friendly positions may prove highly demanding. Locating the proper enemy targets will also be more difficult, and the obstructions due to multistory structures will hamper both sensor and weapon line-of-sight. Techniques such as overlaying tactical charts and local street maps may prove useful in identifying enemy and friendly positions. CAS in an urban environment requires increased reliance on friendly ground forces to locate and mark targets, since enemy combat units will often be concealed inside buildings. Aircrew will have to give extra attention to the axis of attack and target designation; the problem may be similar to attacking enemy forces in steep mountainous terrain. Larger urban areas with more vertically developed buildings add increased elevation issues to the targeting problem, and the combination of tall buildings and narrow streets can cause an "urban canyon" effect leading to masking issues for line-of-sight munitions and targeting sensors. Munitions effects will vary greatly depending on whether the enemy can be attacked in the open versus inside buildings, requiring both patience and flexibility for mission success. When performing CAS in an urban environment, buildings may interfere with communications between air and ground, complicating the coordination process. Ground forces may also have difficulty marking targets for CAS aircraft in an urban environment, and careful consideration must be given to the type of terminal attack control selected. The AC-130 gunship and PGM-equipped fighters using small diameter munitions have proven particularly effective in many urban operations with their combination of precision accuracy and wide range of onboard sensors. The AC-130 and MQ-1 Predator have been useful in urban environments, where extended loiter times are often necessary to pinpoint target sets in close proximity to noncombatants.

Irregular Warfare

Unless specifically stated otherwise, Air Force doctrine applies to the full range of military operations. Irregular warfare, as of the date of this document, is not defined in Air Force or Joint publications. If it is to follow the concept for irregular *forces* defined in JP 1-02, irregular warfare may be defined as warfare performed by armed individuals or groups who are not members of the regular armed forces, police, or other internal security forces. Irregular warfare is not urban warfare, and may or may not be conducted in that environment. Because they share similar challenges, the misuse of terminology is easy to make. Like urban warfare, irregular warfare will likely have increased levels of deception, proximity and confusion with noncombatants, restrictive rules of engagement, and reduced ability to mass forces upon the enemy. In irregular warfare, technologically superior forces can be challenged by an elusive adversary that refuses to mass, and adapts to target the superior force asymmetrically. The primary distinction to be drawn is that irregular *warfare* is conducted by irregular *forces*. Irregular warfare includes a wide variety of operations and activities that occur either in isolation or within traditional types of operations (see AFDD 2).

Within irregular warfare, there are two general approaches: waging irregular warfare (primarily offensive in nature) and countering irregular threats (primarily defensive in nature). While they appear to represent two opposite ends of the spectrum, they do share similarities: they both include protraction, intertwining military and non-military methods, participation by violent individuals and groups that do not belong to the regular armed forces or police of any state, and a struggle for control or influence over, and the support of, the host population.

Weaponeering and Allocation

Weaponeering is the process of estimating the quantity and types of lethal and nonlethal weapons needed to achieve desired effects against specific targets. Weaponeering considers such things as the desired effects against the target (both direct weapons effects and indirect desired outcomes), target vulnerability, delivery accuracy, damage criteria, and weapon reliability. Targeting personnel quantify the expected results of lethal and nonlethal weapons employment against prioritized targets to produce desired effects.

Weapons effects are always a critical part of targeting for counterland. Some munitions and fuses are designed for very specific applications and are effective against certain targets with little or no capability against others. Good intelligence data on target information is vital to the proper matching of munition to target. Likewise, the flexibility of some munitions and fuses to provide multiple effects allows planners options for maximum effect against preplanned targets, and in many cases allows inflight selection of weapons/fuse settings for dynamic targets. The latter capability is especially important for CAS and XAI, when the specific target type is not normally known prior to takeoff. When possible, combat aircraft should have a variety of munitions to meet operational requirements.

Allocation is the distribution of limited resources among competing requirements for employment. Allocation assigns specific air assets and targets against the apportionment priorities. After allocation, the master air attack plan is created that matches assets against AI and strategic targets. Following allocation, the distribution process matches CAS assets against support requests, which should be planned by the ASOC in conjunction with ground force planning. The final step of the process is the actual ATO production, which packages the attacking and supporting assets to achieve optimum effect against the enemy.

AI targets nominated by the ground component are not often presented in the standardized "basic encyclopedia" (BE) number designation, which is another reason to retain flexibility in counterland planning. If the ground component needs a particular enemy unit attacked, and that unit meets the requisite priority criteria, planners must ensure that particular enemy unit is affected to the level required. This requires the CAOC planners to maintain awareness of that enemy unit's position; the BCD can help with this task. Instead of concern over a particular enemy unit, the ground component may have a certain geographic area of concern to its scheme of maneuver. In this case, the friendly ground force requires an attack on any enemy forces that happen to be there. Planning methods must therefore allow for either an area or unit-specific focus for AI targeting, especially for ground-nominated targets. Attacks against large ground forces are most effective when prioritized targeting guidance is included in the nomination, such as artillery first, armor second, etc. When possible, however, air support can be most effective when the ground component specifies mission-type orders or desired effects against an enemy unit, such as "delay enemy X Brigade 72 hours from achieving contact" or "fix enemy Y Division in place for 48 hours." The air-ground system works best when the ground component requests overall battlefield effects, rather than specific targets, due to the greater ability of the air component to analyze the enemy force for proper air and space power targeting.

Before the actual ATO is put into production, justified changes to targets and targeting priority can be incorporated. Once the ATO is put into final production, approved changes are typically passed on to the combat operations division for incorporation either at tactical unit level planning or during actual mission execution. If the enemy ground force does move to an unexpected location, it is not likely to have moved far enough to require much repackaging of counterland missions. This allows for a relatively simple retargeting of a given flight or strike package to the new target location. Any changes must account for differing air defenses, proximity to friendly ground forces, and other factors before final approval.

For those missions where lucrative targets are highly likely, but preplanned locations are not available, airborne or ground alert may be appropriate. This is the most common method employed for CAS, where there is typically not a pre-identified target prior to mission execution. Airborne alert AI can be used to provide up-to-the-minute flexibility, where final targeting guidance comes from offboard sources such as JSTARS or UA. Airborne alert missions should only be planned when lucrative targets are likely to exist, otherwise the missions will be wasted. The "push" system of providing preplanned backup targets for both CAS and AI alleviates this problem to some extent; this procedure gives each mission a fixed target of some military value in case the primary target fails to materialize.

EXECUTION PLANNING AND FORCE EXECUTION

Execution planning includes the preparation necessary for combat units to accomplish the decentralized execution of the ATO. It generally consists of the 12 hours immediately prior to the start of a given day's ATO execution period. Force execution refers to the 24-hour period in which a particular ATO is executed by combat units. The CAOC assists in preparing input for, supporting, and monitoring execution. This section briefly touches on these topics to make the reader aware of its connection with counterland operations. For more information, see AFDD 2-1.9, *Targeting*.

During execution, the CAOC is the central agency for revising the tasking of air and space forces. It is also responsible for coordinating and deconflicting any changes with appropriate agencies or components. Due to battlespace dynamics, the CFACC may be required to make changes to planned operations during execution. The CAOC must be flexible and responsive to changes required during execution of the ATO. Forces not apportioned for joint or combined operations, but included on the ATO for coordination purposes, can be redirected only with the approval of the respective component or allied commanders. During execution, the CFACC is also responsible for retargeting air assets to respond to moving targets or changing priorities.

Dynamic targeting includes the prosecution of targets that emerge during ATO execution that commanders deem worthy of prosecution. The dynamic targeting process is not separate from the air tasking cycle or planned targeting process and is time-sensitive to some degree. The combat operations division (COD) has overall responsibility for implementation of the dynamic targeting process. Successful dynamic targeting, however, requires a great deal of prior planning and coordination with other divisions within the CAOC and with other components. If dynamic targeting is to be done correctly, planners must decide upon CONOPS that make assets available to the COD prior to the start of execution. This can be done in a number of ways. Among the most common methods are:

- ✪ Preplanned target reference methods and FSCM such as kill boxes.

- ✪ Pre-positioned or on-call ISR and strike packages for rapid response to emerging targets.

- ✪ Using intelligence preparation of the operational environment (IPOE) to determine the most probable areas where targets will emerge during execution.

- ✪ Coordination and synchronization of dynamic targeting operations by streamlining and developing procedures for rapid handover of the mission tasking to another component for mission execution if the air and space component cannot attack a target that emerges.

LNOs from other components or Services may be very helpful during the dynamic targeting process. LNOs—particularly the SOLE—may be able to provide the CFACC with additional options for dealing with emerging targets and may be able to provide locations and activities of SOF and other friendly forces to assist with the F2T2EA of counterland targets, or to at least assist in deconfliction.

AIR-GROUND INTEGRATION

A quick survey of the various types of ground maneuver reveals some insight as to how counterland operations should be employed when directly supporting the ground battle. The same survey yields some lessons for employing ground forces when air and space power provides the bulk of battlefield effects on the enemy. The important question does not focus on which component is the more decisive, but how best to combine the available air and surface combat power for the quickest and most cost effective victory.

During the movement to contact by ground forces, the initial combat between friendly and enemy units will occur using supporting air assets and artillery. Counterland's main contribution during this phase is AI—to disrupt the enemy forces that will subsequently be engaged by friendly ground units, or to destroy them prior to contact. Enemy second echelon forces are also valuable targets in this phase, when AI seeks to isolate the enemy front-line units from their support and reinforcements. Ground forces may make good use of organic rotary-wing assets to screen ahead and to the flanks during movement to contact, a task that can be supplemented by fixed-wing counterland assets when needed.

Meeting engagements occur when friendly and enemy ground forces engage while both are on the move. Hasty attacks occur with little time for detailed planning, typically within 24 hours of first contact with the enemy. In both of these modes of ground combat, there may not be time for the normal target nomination and air component apportionment processes to occur before missions must be flown. Depending on the amount of air support required, and other theater priorities for air and space power, missions may be diverted or reroled to fly CAS or AI missions. Since preplanned targets may not be available, counterland assets may be forced into greater use of airborne alert or general grid box target locations for AI missions. Flexibility will be paramount because enemy vulnerabilities that are susceptible to air attack may appear on short notice. Under these circumstances, it is especially important for the ASOC and TACPs to remain tightly integrated with their ground component counterparts, as confusion over both friendly and enemy troop positions and movements is likely.

A hasty ground engagement may often be the result of a desire to attack quickly to surprise the enemy, so they will likely be suffering from the same short-notice reaction that affects friendly planning and air-ground coordination. When significant friendly counterland assets are not available or when air superiority has not been achieved, the friendly ground force should be cautious about schemes of maneuver that increase the likelihood of meeting engagements or hasty attacks, unless sufficient organic surface firepower exists to deal with the enemy force.

A deliberate attack occurs when adequate time for planning and coordination exists; this is the preferred mode of ground advance. Air and ground components will have time for properly detailed coordination, establish on-call FSCLs, nominate appropriate AI targets to achieve desired battlefield results, and ensure air superiority that minimizes the enemy's use of air to support their own army.

Exploitation of breakthroughs into the enemy rear, potentially combined with the use of airborne or air assault forces, achieves maximum disruption when combined with counterland aerial maneuver. Integrated air-ground operations against the enemy, possibly over a multi-phased offensive, require the advanced planning that only a deliberate attack provides. The need for both flexibility and close coordination between air and ground components grows as friendly ground forces push deeper into enemy territory. The rate of ground advance must continually be balanced with the effectiveness of air attack in achieving theater objectives and with the relative merits of ground versus air and space maneuver as they come into play. Proper advancement of the FSCL is one of the key issues during rapid ground advance as the factors of air and space power effectiveness, potential fratricide, and freedom of ground maneuver are weighed.

A spoiling attack is launched from a defensive position to disrupt a forming enemy offensive and may act to divert enemy attention from the main ground offensive to be launched elsewhere. Since disruption of the enemy is the main objective, the use of counterland can contribute greatly to success. Enemy forces may be particularly vulnerable while marshalling for an attack, and second-echelon forces may be more vulnerable to AI while moving up to reinforce an enemy offensive. Successful interdiction of enemy exploitation forces may persuade the enemy to call off an attack, since they would then have no ground force to consolidate any gains.

Mobile defense is a concept in which friendly ground forces use fire and movement tactics over a given area to slow and disrupt the enemy advance. Air and space power's greatest contribution to mobile defense may be with AI close to the battlefield to slow the enemy's movement through destruction of POL, lines of communication, and other infrastructure targets whose destruction will guarantee that friendly ground forces retain greater mobility than the enemy. In mobile defense both the friendly and enemy positions can become difficult to accurately track, and the ASOCs and TACPs again become a critical link when heavy CAS is required. The risk of fratricide will increase during mobile operations, so organic surface firepower should always be used when available.

Area defense is more static and involves a direct confrontation with the enemy along a defensible line of contact. Under these circumstances counterland missions can be flown in closer proximity to ground forces with reduced chance of fratricide, and the more static nature of the conflict will reduce the impact of attacks on enemy mobility. Enemy ammunition stocks, artillery tubes, and rocket launchers may become higher priority targets for AI and CAS during area defense. If air superiority is challenged or lost, friendly surface forces in static positions will likely become very vulnerable to enemy air and missile attack, since fixed ground positions are vulnerable to a lower level of air and space technology than mobile forces.

Target defenses may distract aircrews and hamper their ability to identify and attack targets. Detection assets like JSTARS, or intelligence sources such as human and imagery intelligence will often enhance target acquisition capability. However, enemy air defenses may still hamper the aircrews' ability to visually acquire their targets, due to required high speeds, low or very high altitudes, or restricted ingress routing necessary to minimize the risk of engagement. Effective force packaging can negate the impact of enemy air defenses and achieve temporary local air superiority. A longer-lasting effect is achieved by first eliminating or negating enemy surface-to-air defenses as part of an overall air superiority operation. Many current SEAD assets are multirole, and once the bulk of the enemy surface-to-air defense has been eliminated these forces can be reroled into the main counterland effort. Missions against CAS targets can often use ground force artillery, rockets, and attack helicopters to suppress enemy air defenses, which also free fixed-wing assets to directly attack the primary targets. The ground component also possesses a limited capability to suppress enemy air defenses at longer ranges through the use of ATACMS and attack helicopter assets.

SUMMARY

It cannot be overemphasized that proper counterland planning, as with all air component planning, requires a full consideration of the capabilities and limitations of air and space power during the initial development of overall theater strategy. Historically, theater campaign planners have taken a land-centric view of how the campaign should unfold through its various phases, then examined how airpower would support it. This approach is inefficient, especially in light of the fact that in recent campaigns, airpower has been responsible for damaging or destroying the majority of enemy systems.

True joint planning requires that all components be equally involved in planning the various stages of a military campaign. How counterland fits into the larger picture of a specific strategy will depend on numerous variables, but there should be no preconceived notions about the decisiveness of any one component. Instead of individual component decisiveness, it is better to plan in terms of the required components of a decisive joint force. Likewise, friction and the fog of war should never be ruled out. Any plan that assumes perfect knowledge of the enemy is doomed to failure; proper counterland planning must provide some last-minute flexibility for reaction to unanticipated enemy movement.

Counterland requires effective training and education to ensure success in war. "Train like you fight" is the prevailing training philosophy in the United States Air Force. This strongly applies to counterland operations because the various interconnected parts that comprise this capability must be trained and thoroughly exercised by all parties if success in combat is to be achieved. AI requires accurate intelligence, thorough planning, and flexible execution to achieve desired effects, whether conducted independently or indirectly supporting surface forces. The orchestration required by the air and ground components in the CAS environment can make it one of the most difficult missions performed by the Air Force. To integrate effectively within the combined force, Airmen must accomplish realistic training scenarios, share ideas within the joint community, and advocate the proper use of counterland air and space power. Only then will the investment of peacetime preparation pay exponential dividends during combat.

SU□□□S□□□ R□A□□□□S

A□□□□□□ □□□□□□□□□□□ (Note: All Air Force doctrine documents are available on the Air Force Doctrine Center web page at: https://www.doctrine.af.mil)

AFDD 1, *Air Force Basic Doctrine*

AFDD 2, *Organization and Employment of Aerospace Power*

AFDD 2-1, *Air Warfare*

AFDD 2-1.9, *Targeting*

□□□□□□□□□□□□□□□□

Joint Pub 3-03, *Doctrine for Joint Interdiction Operations*

Joint Pub 3-06, *Doctrine for Joint Urban Operations*

Joint Pub 3-09.3, *Joint Tactics, Techniques, and Procedures for Close Air Support (CAS)*

A□□□□□□ S□□ A□□□□□□□□ □A□SA□□□□□□□□□□□□— available on their website: https://wwwmil.alsa.mil/index.html)

AFTTP(I) 3-2.29, *Multi-Service Tactics, Techniques, and Procedures (MTTP) for Aviation Urban Operations*

AFTTP(I) 3-2.6, *MTTP for Joint Application of Firepower (JFIRE)*

AFTTP(I) 3-2.59, *MTTP for Kill box Employment (Kill Box)*

AFTTP(I) 3-2.17, *MTTP for the Theater Air Ground System (TAGS)*

AFTTP(I) 3-2.3, *MTTP for Time-Sensitive Targets (TST)*

□ □□□□□□□□□□□□□□□□

Cohen, Eliot A. & Keaney, Thomas A. *Revolution in Warfare? Air Power in the Persian Gulf.* Naval Institute Press, 1995.

Clodfelter, Mark. *The Limits of Airpower: The American Bombing of North Vietnam.* New York: The Free Press, 1989.

Cooling, Benjamin F. (ed.) *Case Studies in the Development of Close Air Support.* Office of Air Force History, 1990.

Deichmann, Paul & Price, Alfred. (ed.) *Spearhead For Blitzkrieg.* New York: Ivy Books, 1999.

Drew, Dennis M. "US Airpower Theory and the Insurgent Challenge: A Short Journey to Confusion." *The Journal of Military History 62,* (October 1998): 809-32.

Eduard, Mark. *Aerial Interdiction in Three Wars.* Center for Air Force History, 1994.

Fadok, Lt Col David S. "John Boyd and John Warden: Airpower's Quest for Strategic Paralysis." In *Paths of Heaven: The Evolution of Airpower Theory.* Edited by Col (Ret) Phillip S. Meilinger. Maxwell AFB: Air University Press, 1997.

Futrell, Robert F. *The United States Air Force in Korea.* Office of Air Force History, 1983.

Gilster, Herman L. The *Air War in Southeast Asia: Case Studies of Selected Campaigns.* Maxwell AFB: Air University Press, 1993.

Givens, Robert P. *Turning the Vertical Flank: Airpower as a Maneuver Force in the Theater Campaign.* Maxwell AFB: Air University Press, 2002.

Grant, Rebecca. *Gulf War II: Air and Space Power Led the Way.* Air Force Association Special Report, September 2003. Arlington: Aerospace Education Foundation, 2003.

Hosmer, Stephen T. *Psychological Effects of U.S. Air Operations in Four Wars 1941-1994: Lessons for U.S. Commanders.* Santa Monica: RAND, 1996.

Hughes, Thomas A. *OVERLORD: General Pete Quesada and the Triumph of Tactical Air Power in World War II.* Free Press, 1995.

Kennett, Lee. *The First Air War.* Smithsonian, 1991.

Kenney, George C. *General Kenney Reports.* Office of Air Force History, 1987 (originally published in 1949).

Lambeth, Benjamin S. *NATO's Air War for Kosovo: A Strategic and Operational Assessment.* Santa Monica: RAND, 2001.

Mets, David R. *The Air Campaign: John Warden and the Classical Airpower Theorists.* Maxwell AFB: Air University Press, 1999.

Pape, Robert A. *Bombing to Win: Airpower and Coercion in War.* Ithaca: Cornell University Press, 1996.

Rudel, Hans Ulrich. *Stuka Pilot.* Bantam, 1979 (first published in US by Ballantine in 1958).

Slessor, J.C. *Air Power and Armies.* Oxford University Press, 1936.

Thompson, Wayne. *To Hanoi and Back: The USAF and North Vietnam, 1966-1973.* Washington: Air Force History and Museums Program, 2000.

Warden III, John A.. *The Air Campaign: Planning for Combat.* Fort McNair: National Defense University Press, 1988.

□□□SSARY

A□□□□□□□□□□ □□□ A□□□□□ □

A□□□	Army airspace command and control
AA□S	Army air-ground system
A□A	airspace control authority
A□□□	air component coordination element
A□M	airspace control measure
A□□	airspace control order
A□AR□	Air Force air request net
A□□□	Air Force doctrine document
A□	air interdiction
A□□	air liaison officer
A□SA	Air Land Sea Application (Center)
A□	area of operations
A□□	air and space operations center
ARS	area reference system
AS□□	air support operations center
AS□□	air support operations group
ASR	air support request
A□A□MS	Army tactical missile system
A□□	air tasking order
A□ A□S	airborne warning and control system
□A□□	battalion air liaison officer
□□□	battlefield coordination detachment
□□□	battlefield coordination line
□□□	brigade combat team
□□A	battle damage assessment
□□	basic encyclopedia
□□	command and control
□A□□	combined air and space operations center
□AS	close air support
□□□	collateral damage estimate
□□A□□	combined force air and space component commander
□□□	coordinated fire lines
□□□	combat identification
□□	coordination line
□□□	combat operations division
□□MA□□□R	commander, Air Force forces
□□MAR□□R	Commander, Army forces
□□□□□S	concept of operations
□R□	control and reporting center

□SAR	combat search and rescue
□AS□	direct air support center
□□□	expeditionary operations center
□□	electronic warfare
□A□	forward air controller
□A□□A□	forward air controller, airborne
□□	forward boundary
□□□□A	forward edge of the battle area
□□A	free fire area
□□□□	forward line of the troops
□M	field manual
□□□	forward operating base
□S□□	fire support coordination line
□S□M	fire support coordination measure
□□□□□A	find, fix, track, target, engage and assess
□A□	ground alert, air interdiction
□ARS	global area reference system
□□AS	ground alert, close air support
□□□	ground liaison officer
□□S	global positioning system
□AM	inertially guided munitions
□□	information operations
□□□□	intelligence preparation of the operational environment
□R	infrared
□SR	intelligence, surveillance, and reconnaissance
□A□□	Joint air control element
□A□□□	joint air-ground control cell
□A□□	joint air and space operations center
□A□□	joint air and space operations plan
□AR□	joint air request net
□□AM	joint direct attack munitions
□□A□□	joint force air and space component commander
□□□	joint force commander
□□□R□	Multi-Service Procedures for the Joint Application of Firepower
□□□□□	joint force land component commander
□□□	joint fires observer
□□S□□□	joint force special operations component commander
□□□□□	joint integrated prioritized target list
□□A	joint operations area

□□	joint publication
□S□A□□	joint special operations air component commander
□S□ARS	Joint Surveillance Target Attack Radar System
□□A□	joint terminal attack controller
□□□□	joint targeting coordination board
□□	kilometer
□□□□□	low-density, high-demand
□□□	lines of communications
□□□	liaison officer
MA□□S	Marine air command and control system
MA□□□	Marine air ground task force
MAR□□	Marine liaison officer
M□□□	multi-Service tactics, techniques, and procedures
□A□□	naval and amphibious liaison element
□A□□	North Atlantic Treaty Organization
□□A	no-fire area
□□A□S	Navy tactical air control system
□□□	Operation IRAQI FREEDOM
□□□□□	operational control
□□□R□	operations order
□A	public affairs
□□M	precision-guided munitions
□□	probability of incapacitation
□□□	positive identification
□□□	petroleum, oils, and lubricants
□SY□□	psychological operations
RA□	Royal Air Force (UK)
R□A	restricted fire area
R□□	rules of engagement
R□□	restricted operating zone
S□AR	strike coordination and reconnaissance
S□A□	suppression of enemy air defense
S□□	special operations forces
S□□□	special operations liaison element
S□□S	special instructions
S□□	special tactics team

□A□A□	tactical air coordinator, airborne
□A□□	tactical air control center (US Navy and USMC)
□A□□□	tactical control
□A□□	tactical air control parties
□A□S	theater air control system
□A□□	tactical air direction center
□A□S	theater air ground system
□□M□S	theater battle management core systems
□□□	troops-in-contact
□S□	time-sensitive targets
□□□	tactics, techniques, and procedures
UA	unmanned aircraft
UAS	unmanned aerial system
USAA□	United States Army Air Forces
□ □S□□□	World Geodetic System 1984
□ M□	weapons of mass destruction
□ □□	wing operations center
□A□	airborne alert, air interdiction
□□AS	airborne alert, close air support

□ □□□□□□□

□□□ □□□□□□□□□□□Air operations conducted to destroy, neutralize, or delay the enemy's military potential before it can be brought to bear effectively against friendly forces at such distance from friendly forces that detailed integration of each air mission with the fire and movement of friendly forces is not required. (JP 1-02) [*Air operations conducted to divert, disrupt, delay, or destroy the enemy's military potential before it can be brought to bear effectively against friendly forces, or to otherwise achieve joint force commander objectives. Air interdiction is conducted at such distance from friendly forces that detailed integration of each air mission with the fire and movement of friendly forces is not required. Also called AI.*] [AFDD 2-1.3] {Words in brackets apply only to the Air Force and are offered for clarity.}

□□□ □□□□□□ □□□□□□□The senior tactical air control party member attached to a ground unit who functions as the primary advisor to the ground commander on air power. An air liaison officer is usually an aeronautically rated officer. Also called A□□ (JP 1-02)

□□□□□ □□□□□□□□□□□□□A compilation of identified installations and physical areas

96

of potential significance as objectives for attack. Also called ⬚⬚⬚(JP 1-02)

⬚⬚⬚⬚⬚⬚⬚⬚⬚⬚A line that delineates surface areas for the purpose of facilitating coordination and deconfliction of operations between adjacent units, formations, or areas. (JP 1-02)

⬚⬚⬚ ⬚⬚⬚⬚⬚⬚A series of related military operations aimed at accomplishing a strategic or operational objective within a given time and space. (JP 1-02)

⬚⬚⬚ ⬚⬚⬚⬚⬚ ⬚⬚⬚⬚⬚A plan for a series of related military operations aimed at accomplishing a strategic or operational objective within a given time and space. (JP 1-02)

⬚⬚⬚⬚⬚ ⬚⬚⬚ ⬚⬚⬚⬚⬚⬚⬚⬚⬚Air action by fixed- and rotary-wing aircraft against hostile targets that are in close proximity to friendly forces and that require detailed integration of each air mission with the fire and movement of those forces. Also called ⬚AS⬚(JP 1-02)

⬚⬚⬚⬚⬚ ⬚⬚⬚⬚⬚⬚ ⬚⬚⬚⬚ As used in relation to close air support, close proximity refers to the distance within which some form of terminal attack control is required for targeting direction and fratricide prevention. (AFDD 2-1.3)

⬚⬚⬚⬚⬚⬚⬚⬚⬚⬚⬚Air and space operations against enemy land force capabilities to create effects that achieve joint force commander objectives. The main objectives of counterland operations are to dominate the surface environment and prevent the opponent from doing the same. (AFDD 1)

⬚⬚⬚⬚⬚⬚⬚ ⬚⬚⬚⬚⬚⬚⬚⬚⬚⬚⬚As used in relation to close air support (CAS), detailed integration refers to the level of coordination required to achieve the desired effects without overly restricting CAS attacks, surface firepower, or the ground scheme of maneuver. It is also necessary to protect aircraft from the unintended effects of friendly surface fire. The maximum range requiring detailed integration is typically bounded by the range at which organic surface firepower provides the preponderance of effect on the enemy. (AFDD 2-1.3)

⬚⬚⬚⬚ ⬚⬚⬚ ⬚⬚⬚⬚⬚⬚⬚⬚⬚⬚⬚⬚An officer (aviator/pilot) member of the tactical air control party who, from a forward ground or airborne position, controls aircraft in close air support of ground troops. Also called ⬚A⬚⬚(JP 1-02)

⬚⬚⬚⬚ ⬚⬚⬚ ⬚⬚⬚ ⬚⬚⬚⬚⬚⬚⬚⬚ ⬚⬚⬚⬚⬚⬚⬚⬚⬚A specifically trained and qualified aviation officer who exercises control from the air of aircraft engaged in close air support of ground troops. The forward air controller (airborne) is normally an airborne extension of the tactical air control party. Also called ⬚A⬚A⬚⬚(JP 1-02)

⬚⬚⬚⬚⬚⬚⬚⬚⬚⬚⬚The employment of weapons by friendly forces which results in the unintentional death, injury, or damage to US, allied, or coalition personnel, equipment, or facilities. (AFDD 2-1.3)

□□□□□□□□□□□An action to divert, disrupt, delay, or destroy the enemy's surface military potential before it can be used effectively against friendly forces. See also □□□ □□□□□□□□□□□□(JP 1-02) [*Interdiction operations are joint actions to divert, disrupt, delay, or destroy the enemy's military potential before it can be used effectively against friendly forces, or to otherwise meet joint force commander objectives.*] (AFDD 2-1.3)

□□□□□□Connotes activities, operations, organizations, etc., in which elements of two or more Military Departments participate. (JP 1-02)

□□□□□□ □□□□□□□□□Fundamental principles that guide the employment of US military forces in coordinated action toward a common objective. Joint doctrine contained in joint publications also includes terms, tactics, techniques, and procedures. It is authoritative but requires judgment in application. (JP 1-02)

□□□□□ □□□□□□Fires produced during the employment of forces from two or more components in coordinated action toward a common objective. (JP 1-02)

□□□□□ □□□□□ □□□□□□□□□□A trained Service member who can request, adjust, and control surface-to-surface fires, provide targeting information in support of type 2 and 3 close air support terminal attack controls, and perform autonomous terminal guidance operations. Also called □□□ □(USA, USAF, USSOCOM 14 Nov 05 MOA) [The intent of a JFO is to add joint warfighting capability, not circumvent the need for qualified JTACs.] (AFDD 2-1.3) See also type 1, 2, and 3 terminal control.

□□□□□ □□□□□ □□□ □□□ □□□□□□ □□□ □ □□□□□□ The commander within a unified command, subordinate unified command, or joint task force responsible to the establishing commander for making recommendations on the proper employment of assigned, attached, and/or made available for tasking air forces; planning and coordinating air operations; or accomplishing such operational missions as may be assigned. The joint force air component commander is given the authority necessary to accomplish missions and tasks assigned by the establishing commander. Also called □□A□□□(JP 1-02) *[The joint air and space component commander (JFACC) uses the joint air and space operations center to command and control the integrated air and space effort to meet the joint force commander's objectives. This title emphasizes the Air Force position that air power and space power together create effects that cannot be achieved through air or space power alone.]* [AFDD 2] {Words in brackets apply only to the Air Force and are offered for clarity.}

□□□□□ □□□□□ □□□ □ □□□□□□A general term applied to a combatant commander, subunified commander, or joint task force commander authorized to exercise combatant command (command authority) or operational control over a joint

force. Also called ▢▢▢▢(JP 1-02)

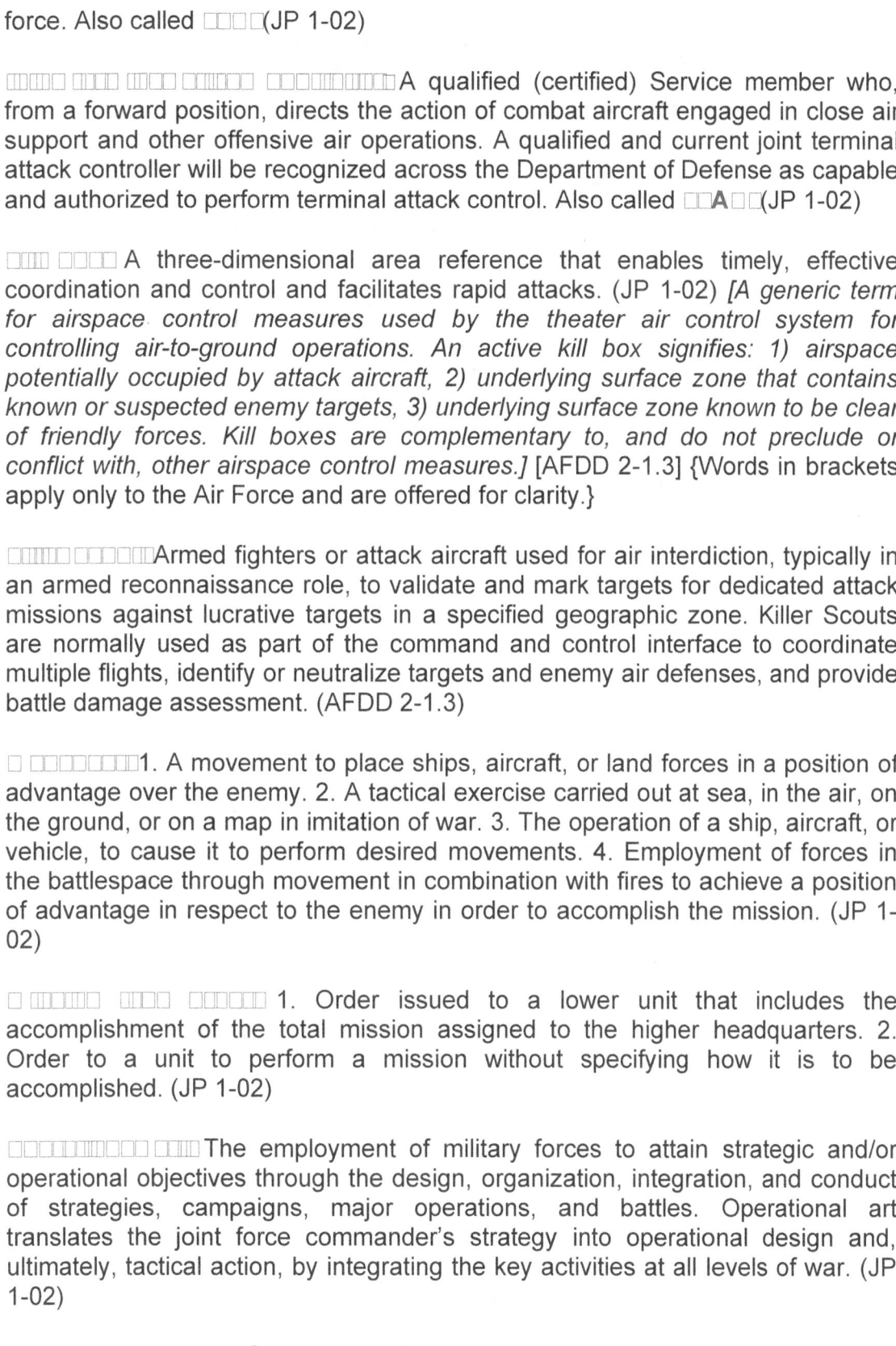

▢▢▢▢▢ ▢▢▢▢ ▢▢▢▢ ▢▢▢▢▢▢ ▢▢▢▢▢▢▢▢▢▢A qualified (certified) Service member who, from a forward position, directs the action of combat aircraft engaged in close air support and other offensive air operations. A qualified and current joint terminal attack controller will be recognized across the Department of Defense as capable and authorized to perform terminal attack control. Also called ▢▢**A**▢▢(JP 1-02)

▢▢▢▢ ▢▢▢▢ A three-dimensional area reference that enables timely, effective coordination and control and facilitates rapid attacks. (JP 1-02) *[A generic term for airspace control measures used by the theater air control system for controlling air-to-ground operations. An active kill box signifies: 1) airspace potentially occupied by attack aircraft, 2) underlying surface zone that contains known or suspected enemy targets, 3) underlying surface zone known to be clear of friendly forces. Kill boxes are complementary to, and do not preclude or conflict with, other airspace control measures.]* [AFDD 2-1.3] {Words in brackets apply only to the Air Force and are offered for clarity.}

▢▢▢▢▢▢ ▢▢▢▢▢▢Armed fighters or attack aircraft used for air interdiction, typically in an armed reconnaissance role, to validate and mark targets for dedicated attack missions against lucrative targets in a specified geographic zone. Killer Scouts are normally used as part of the command and control interface to coordinate multiple flights, identify or neutralize targets and enemy air defenses, and provide battle damage assessment. (AFDD 2-1.3)

▢ ▢▢▢▢▢▢▢▢▢1. A movement to place ships, aircraft, or land forces in a position of advantage over the enemy. 2. A tactical exercise carried out at sea, in the air, on the ground, or on a map in imitation of war. 3. The operation of a ship, aircraft, or vehicle, to cause it to perform desired movements. 4. Employment of forces in the battlespace through movement in combination with fires to achieve a position of advantage in respect to the enemy in order to accomplish the mission. (JP 1-02)

▢ ▢▢▢▢▢▢ ▢▢▢▢ ▢▢▢▢▢▢ 1. Order issued to a lower unit that includes the accomplishment of the total mission assigned to the higher headquarters. 2. Order to a unit to perform a mission without specifying how it is to be accomplished. (JP 1-02)

▢▢▢▢▢▢▢▢▢▢▢ ▢▢▢▢ The employment of military forces to attain strategic and/or operational objectives through the design, organization, integration, and conduct of strategies, campaigns, major operations, and battles. Operational art translates the joint force commander's strategy into operational design and, ultimately, tactical action, by integrating the key activities at all levels of war. (JP 1-02)

▢▢▢▢▢▢▢▢▢▢▢▢▢▢▢▢▢▢▢Command authority that may be exercised by commanders at any echelon at or below the level of combatant command. Operational control is inherent in combatant command (command authority) and may be delegated within the command. When forces are transferred between combatant commands, the command relationship the gaining commander will exercise (and the losing commander will relinquish) over these forces must be specified by the Secretary of Defense. Operational control is the authority to perform those functions of command over subordinate forces involving organizing and employing commands and forces, assigning tasks, designating objectives, and giving authoritative direction necessary to accomplish the mission. Operational control includes authoritative direction over all aspects of military operations and joint training necessary to accomplish missions assigned to the command. Operational control should be exercised through the commanders of subordinate organizations. Normally this authority is exercised through subordinate joint force commanders and Service and/or functional component commanders. Operational control normally provides full authority to organize commands and forces and to employ those forces as the commander in operational control considers necessary to accomplish assigned missions; it does not, in and of itself, include authoritative direction for logistics or matters of administration, discipline, internal organization, or unit training. Also called □□□□□□(JP 1-02)

□□□□□□□□□□ □□□□□ □□ □ □□□The level of war at which campaigns and major operations are planned, conducted, and sustained to accomplish strategic objectives within theaters or other operational areas. Activities at this level link tactics and strategy by establishing operational objectives needed to accomplish the strategic objectives, sequencing events to achieve the operational objectives, initiating actions, and applying resources to bring about and sustain these events. These activities imply a broader dimension of time or space than do tactics; they ensure the logistic and administrative support of tactical forces, and provide the means by which tactical successes are exploited to achieve strategic objectives. See also □□□□□□□ □□□□□□□ □□□□□□□□□□□□□ □□□(JP 1-02)

□□□□□□□□□□□□ □□□□□□□□□□□Planned operations to convey selected information and indicators to foreign audiences to influence their emotions, motives, objective reasoning, and ultimately the behavior of foreign governments, organizations, groups, and individuals. The purpose of psychological operations is to induce or reinforce foreign attitudes and behavior favorable to the originator's objectives. Also called □SY□□□(JP 1-02)

□□□□□□□ □□□□□□□□□□ Operations conducted in hostile, denied, or politically sensitive environments to achieve military, diplomatic, informational, and/or economic objectives employing military capabilities for which there is no broad conventional force requirement. These operations often require covert, clandestine, or low visibility capabilities. Special operations are applicable across the range of military operations. They can be conducted independently or in conjunction with operations of conventional forces or other government agencies and may include operations through, with, or by indigenous or surrogate forces.

Special operations differ from conventional operations in degree of physical and political risk, operational techniques, mode of employment, independence from friendly support, and dependence on detailed operational intelligence and indigenous assets. Also called S□□(JP 1-02)

□□□□□□□□□□□□□□□□ □□□□□□ □□□□ □□□□**S**□ □□□□ A special operations liaison team provided by the joint force special operations component commander to the joint force air component commander (if designated), or appropriate Service component air command and control organization, to coordinate, deconflict, and integrate special operations air, surface, and subsurface operations with conventional air operations. (JP 1-02)

□□□□□□□□ □□□□□□□□ □□□The level of war at which a nation, often as a member of a group of nations, determines national or multinational (alliance or coalition) security objectives and guidance, and develops and uses national resources to accomplish these objectives. Activities at this level establish national and multinational military objectives; sequence initiatives; define limits and assess risks for the use of military and other instruments of national power; develop global plans or theater war plans to achieve these objectives; and provide military forces and other capabilities in accordance with strategic plans. See also □□□□□□□□□□□□□□□□ □□□□□□□□□□□□□□□□□ □□(JP 1-02)

□□□□□□□□1. The action of a force that aids, protects, complements, or sustains another force in accordance with a directive requiring such action. 2. A unit that helps another unit in battle. 3. An element of a command that assists, protects, or supplies other forces in combat. See also □□□□□□□□ □□□ □ □□□□□□□□□□□□□ □□□ □ □□□□□□(JP 1-02)

□□□□□□□□ □□□ □ □□□□□□1. The commander having primary responsibility for all aspects of a task assigned by the Joint Strategic Capabilities Plan or other joint operation planning authority. In the context of joint operation planning, this term refers to the commander who prepares operation plans or operation orders in response to requirements of the Chairman of the Joint Chiefs of Staff. 2. In the context of a support command relationship, the commander who receives assistance from another commander's force or capabilities, and who is responsible for ensuring that the supporting commander understands the assistance required. See also □□□□□□□□□□□□□□ □□□ □ □□□□□□(JP 1-02)

□□□□□□□□ □□□ □ □□□□□□1. A commander who provides augmentation forces or other support to a supported commander or who develops a supporting plan. Includes the designated combatant commands and Defense agencies as appropriate. 2. In the context of a support command relationship, the commander who aids, protects, complements, or sustains another commander's force, and who is responsible for providing the assistance required by the supported commander. See also □□□□□□□□□□□□□ □□□ □ □□□□□□(JP 1-02)

⬚⬚⬚⬚⬚⬚⬚⬚⬚⬚⬚⬚⬚⬚ 1. The arrangement of military actions in time, space, and purpose to produce maximum relative combat power at a decisive place and time. 2. In the intelligence context, application of intelligence sources and methods in concert with the operation plan. (JP 1-02)

⬚⬚⬚⬚⬚⬚⬚⬚ ⬚⬚⬚⬚⬚⬚⬚⬚ Command authority over assigned or attached forces or commands, or military capability or forces made available for tasking, that is limited to the detailed direction and control of movements or maneuvers within the operational area necessary to accomplish missions or tasks assigned. Tactical control is inherent in operational control. Tactical control may be delegated to, and exercised at any level at or below the level of combatant command. When forces are transferred between combatant commands, the command relationship the gaining commander will exercise (and the losing commander will relinquish) over these forces must be specified by the Secretary of Defense. Tactical control provides sufficient authority for controlling and directing the application of force or tactical use of combat support assets within the assigned mission or task. Also called ⬚**A**⬚⬚ ⬚⬚See also ⬚⬚⬚⬚⬚⬚⬚⬚⬚⬚⬚⬚⬚⬚⬚⬚⬚⬚ (JP 1-02)

⬚⬚⬚⬚⬚⬚⬚⬚ ⬚⬚⬚⬚⬚⬚⬚⬚⬚⬚ The level of war at which battles and engagements are planned and executed to accomplish military objectives assigned to tactical units or task forces. Activities at this level focus on the ordered arrangement and maneuver of combat elements in relation to each other and to the enemy to achieve combat objectives. See also ⬚⬚⬚⬚⬚⬚⬚⬚⬚⬚⬚⬚⬚⬚⬚⬚⬚⬚ ⬚⬚⬚ ⬚⬚⬚⬚⬚⬚⬚⬚⬚ ⬚⬚⬚⬚⬚ ⬚⬚⬚ ⬚⬚⬚(JP 1-02)

⬚⬚⬚⬚ ⬚⬚⬚⬚ ⬚⬚⬚⬚⬚⬚ ⬚⬚⬚⬚⬚⬚⬚⬚The authority to control the maneuver of and grant weapons release clearance to attacking aircraft. (JP 1-02)

⬚⬚⬚⬚ ⬚⬚⬚⬚⬚⬚⬚⬚⬚ ⬚⬚⬚⬚⬚⬚⬚⬚⬚⬚⬚A qualified officer or enlisted member who, from a forward ground or airborne position, provides terminal control to aircraft performing close air support to ground forces. While terminal attack controllers operate with the ground forces they support, their personnel normally remain under the command of the component providing the close air support. Also called ⬚**A**⬚. (AFDD 2-1.3)

⬚⬚⬚⬚ ⬚⬚⬚⬚⬚⬚⬚⬚⬚⬚⬚⬚⬚1. The authority to direct aircraft to maneuver into a position to deliver ordnance, passengers, or cargo to a specific location or target. Terminal control is a type of air control. 2. Any electronic, mechanical, or visual control given to aircraft to facilitate target acquisition and resolution. (JP 1-02)

⬚⬚⬚⬚ ⬚⬚⬚⬚ ⬚⬚⬚⬚⬚⬚⬚⬚⬚⬚ 1. The guidance applied to a guided missile between midcourse guidance and arrival in the vicinity of the target. 2. Electronic, mechanical, visual, or other assistance given an aircraft pilot to facilitate arrival at, operation within or over, landing upon, or departure from an air landing or airdrop facility. 3. Any electronic, mechanical, voice or visual communication that provides approaching aircraft or weapons additional information regarding a specific location or target. Terminal guidance is not a type of air control. Those providing terminal guidance do not have weapons release authority, or authority to direct the maneuver of aircraft. See also terminal control. (JP 1-02)

🔲🔲🔲🔲 🔲 🔲🔲🔲🔲🔲🔲 Type 1 control is used when the JTAC must visually acquire the attacking aircraft and the target for each attack. Analysis of attacking aircraft geometry is required to reduce the risk of the attack affecting friendly forces. (JP 3-09.3)

🔲🔲🔲🔲 🔲 🔲🔲🔲🔲🔲🔲 Type 2 control will be used when the JTAC requires control of individual attacks but assesses that either visual acquisition of the attacking aircraft or target at weapons release is not possible or when attacking aircraft are not in a position to acquire the mark/target prior to weapons release/ launch. (JP 3-09.3)

🔲🔲🔲🔲 🔲 🔲🔲🔲🔲🔲🔲 Type 3 control is used when the JTAC requires the ability to provide clearance for multiple attacks within a single engagement subject to specific attack restrictions. Type 3 control does not require the JTAC to visually acquire the aircraft or the target; however, all targeting data must be coordinated through the supported commander's battle staff. (JP 3-09.3)

www.ingramcontent.com/pod-product-compliance
Lightning Source LLC
Chambersburg PA
CBHW080304290526
45790CB00005B/1924